Ireland in Conflict 1922–1998

IN THE SAME SERIES

General Editors: Eric J. Evans and P. D. King

LANCASTER PAMPHLETS

Ireland in Conflict
1922–1998

T. G. Fraser

London and New York

First published 2000
by Routledge
11 New Fetter Lane, London EC4P 4EE

Simultaneously published in the USA and Canada
by Routledge
29 West 35th Street, New York, NY 10001

Typeset in Bembo by BC Typesetting, Bristol
Printed and bound in Great Britain by
Clays Ltd, St Ives plc

British Library Cataloguing in Publication Data
A catalogue record for this book is available from the British Library

Library of Congress Cataloguing in Publication Data
Fraser, T.G.
Ireland in conflict 1922–1998/T.G. Fraser.
p.   cm. – (Lancaster pamphlets)
Includes bibliographical references (p.   ).
ISBN 0–415–16549–0
1. Ireland–History–1992–   2. Political violence–Ulster
(Northern Ireland and Ireland)–History–20th century.   3. Social
conflict–Ulster (Northern Ireland and Ireland)–History–20th
century.   4. Northern Ireland–History.   I. Title.   II. Series.
DA963.F73   1999
941.5082–dc21   99–23986
                                                            CIP

ISBN 0–415–16549–0

Contents

Preface

In 1922, Ireland entered a new phase in its national development. The parliamentary Union with Britain, which had come into being on 1 January 1801, came to an end with the creation of the Irish Free State as a Dominion within the British Empire. Although, as will be seen, the Free State was not accepted by everyone who had fought for Irish independence, Ireland's future was to be determined in Dublin, not in London. But not all of Ireland. The Government of Ireland Act of 1920 had already set in place a form of partition with Home Rule, through which six Ulster counties were constituted as a new political entity, Northern Ireland. Although Northern Ireland remained within the United Kingdom, it did so in a rather semi-detached way, with a devolved parliament in Belfast, which made it quite distinct from England, Scotland and Wales. What lay at the heart of that partition hardly needs stating; the resistance of the Protestant Ulster unionists to rule by a Dublin parliament in the years before 1914. Their objections were religious, economic and political. In religious terms, they feared being a permanent minority in a state and parliament inevitably dominated by Ireland's Catholic majority. In economic terms, they saw the industries of Belfast, shipbuilding, engineering, linen and tobacco, suffering under the priorities of a predominantly agrarian Ireland. Their markets lay in Britain and her world empire. Pride in that empire, too, featured in their political sentiments, for this was still the age of imperialism. These sentiments were not shared by the Catholic nationalists of Ulster, who fully identified with Irish national aspirations. The Government of Ireland Act allowed the unionists of Ulster to retain their British links and identity, albeit in a somewhat modified form. It also excluded the nationalists of Ulster from the new Irish state. Here was the chasm, for it was no less than that, which lay at the heart of Irish politics and society from 1922.

Of course, there was infinitely more to Ireland, north and south, than this conflict. A vibrant cultural life went alongside the impulses of a global culture, by the 1930s largely coming from the United States but based on the use of English. One of the most devoutly religious societies in western Europe, Catholic and Protestant, was faced with the challenge of secularisation. Nor could either part of Ireland stand aside from the steady advance of post-war European unity, itself designed by its founding fathers to cut across the national divisions which had led to two world wars in 30 years. Ireland was an island only in the geographical sense, by no means immune to outside political, economic and cultural influences. But the conflict of nationality in Northern Ireland was always there, an insistent counterpoint to whatever else was happening on the island.

It is such matters that this pamphlet attempts to address, though with conflict as its core concern. The first chapters have as their focus the emergence and evolution of the two parts of Ireland down to 1949, examining the key changes in political and constitutional structures. Attention then turns to the accelerating pace of change in the period between 1949 and 1972, by which time the problems of Northern Ireland had become acute, with the breakdown of existing structures. Subsequent chapters concentrate on the Northern Ireland 'Troubles', charting the difficult and violent course of events which culminated in the Good Friday Agreement of 1998. The final chapter summarises some of the main points at issue.

As an historian who has worked at the University of Ulster since 1969, I have had the immeasurable benefit of discussing the events of modern Irish history with a number of colleagues who have contributed more than they may realise. In particular, I am indebted to Paul Arthur, Arthur Aughey, Sean Connolly, Seamus Dunn, Robert Hutchinson, Janice Holmes, Keith Kyle, Brendan Lynn, James Loughlin, Duncan Morrow, Emmet O'Connor, Terry O'Keeffe and Henry Patterson. Dominic Bryan and Neil Jarman, who worked with me on a study of parading controversies, travelled with me to many parts of Northern Ireland, giving many insights into politics on the ground. Heather McCallum of Routledge waited patiently for this pamphlet as critical events in Northern Ireland politics worked themselves out. I am particularly indebted to Grace Fraser and Keith Jeffery who made time in their own busy schedules to read, and improve, my text. The series editors, Eric Evans and David King, also made invaluable comments. Needless to say, I am solely responsible for the interpretation of events, which are, in their nature, controversial.

Crown copyright material is reproduced by permission of the Controller of Her Majesty's Stationery Office.

Chronological table

1922

7 January	Dáil split on Treaty
16 January	Free State ministers enter Dublin Castle
7 April	Special Powers Act introduced in Northern Ireland
14 April	Rory O'Connor seizes Four Courts in Dublin
16 June	Pro-Treaty parties win Free State elections
28 June	Free State forces attack Four Courts
12 August	Death of Griffith
22 August	Death of Collins

1923

8 April	Cosgrave forms Cumann na nGaedheal
30 April	Civil War ends
27 August	Second Free State election

1925

7 November	Boundary Commission proposals leaked to press

1926

16 May	De Valera forms Fianna Fáil

1927

12 August	De Valera and Fianna Fáil take seats in Dáil

1932

9 March   De Valera forms government on winning February election

1935

12 July   Sectarian rioting in Belfast

1937

1 July   Irish Constitution enacted

1939

3 September   Start of Second World War in Europe

1941

15–16 April   German air raid on Belfast
4–5 May   German air raid on Belfast
31 May   German air raid on Dublin

1945

8 May   End of Second World War in Europe

1948

1 September   John A. Costello announces intention to create Republic

1949

June   Ireland Act confirms Northern Ireland's constitutional position

1951

11 April   Resignation of Noel Browne over 'Mother and Child' scheme

1956

11–12 December   Start of IRA campaign; terminated February 1962

1958

12 November   Publication of *Programme for Economic Expansion*, inspired by T. K. Whitaker and implemented by Seán Lemass

1963

25 March   Terence O'Neill becomes Prime Minister of Northern Ireland

1965

14 January   Visit of Seán Lemass to Stormont

1968

5 October   Civil Rights march in Derry
9 December   O'Neill's 'Ulster at the Crossroads' broadcast

1969

1–4 January   People's Democracy march from Belfast to Derry
28 April   Resignation of O'Neill; Chichester-Clark Prime Minister
12–14 August   Apprentice Boys parade, followed by 'Battle of the Bogside' and deployment of British troops
14 August   Disturbances spread to Belfast and other towns
19 August   Downing Street Declaration

1970

11 January   Provisional Republican movement set up after split in Sinn Féin Ard Fheis
21 April   Formation of Alliance Party
3 July   Falls Road curfew
21 August   Formation of Social Democratic and Labour Party

1971

6 February   First British soldier killed by Provisional IRA
20 March   Resignation of Chichester-Clark; succeded by Brian Faulkner
9 August   Internment introduced
30 October   Formation of Democratic Unionist Party by Rev Ian Paisley

1972

30 January   'Bloody Sunday' in Derry
24 March   Northern Ireland parliament suspended
26 June–13 July IRA ceasefire
21 July   'Bloody Friday' bombs in Belfast

| 31 July | Military operation to end 'No Go' areas in Derry and Belfast; Claudy bombing |

1973
| 28 June | Northern Ireland Assembly elections |
| 6 December | Sunningdale Conference |

1974
4 January	Ulster Unionist Council rejects Sunningdale Agreement
14–27 May	Ulster Workers Council strike
17 May	Loyalist bombs kill 22 in Dublin and five in Monaghan
21 November	IRA bombs kill 21 in Birmingham
22 December	Provisional IRA truce

1975
| 17 January | IRA truce ends |
| 10 February | IRA ceasefire; ends 22 September |

1976
| 10 August | Start of Peace People Movement |

1979
27 August	IRA kills Lord Mountbatten near Sligo and 18 soldiers at Warrenpoint
7 September	James Molyneaux becomes Ulster Unionist leader
22 November	John Hume becomes SDLP leader

1981
| 1 March | Bobby Sands begins hunger strike; dies 5 May |
| 3 October | Hunger strikes end after nine more deaths |

1984
2 May	Publication of New Ireland Forum Report
12 October	IRA bomb at Conservative Party Conference
19 November	Margaret Thatcher rejects three Forum options

1985
| 15 November | Margaret Thatcher and Garret FitzGerald sign Anglo-Irish Agreement |

23 November	Mass unionist rally in Belfast against Agreement

1986

2 November	Sinn Féin Ard Fheis votes to end policy of abstention from the Dáil

1987

8 November	IRA bomb kills 11 at Remembrance Day service in Enniskillen

1988

January	Beginning of Hume–Adams dialogue
6 March	Three IRA members killed in Gibraltar, followed by series of deaths in Belfast
1 November	Arms ship *Eksund* intercepted off France

1989

3 November	Peter Brooke indicates possibility of talks with Sinn Féin

1991

26 March	Peter Brooke defines three 'Strands' for future talks

1992

17 January	Seven Protestant workmen killed at Teebane, Co. Tyrone
5 February	Five Catholics killed on Ormeau Road, Belfast
10 April	IRA bombs Baltic Exchange, London

1993

24 April	IRA bombs NatWest Tower, London
23 October	Ten killed in IRA Shankill Road bomb
30 October	Eight killed in UFF Greysteel shooting
15 December	Downing Street Declaration

1994

31 August	IRA announces ceasefire
13 October	Combined Loyalist Military Command announces ceasefire

1995

22 February	Frameworks documents published

9 July	'Siege of Drumcree', Portadown
28 August	James Molyneaux resigns as leader of Ulster Unionist Party; succeeded by David Trimble on 8 September
30 November	President Clinton visits Northern Ireland

1996

22 January	Report of the International Body on arms decommissioning
9 February	IRA ends ceasefire with bomb at Canary Wharf, London
30 May	Elections to Northern Ireland Forum
7 July	Second crisis over Drumcree parade

1997

30 January	Report of the North Committee on parading
1 May	Election of New Labour Government in United Kingdom; Dr Marjorie Mowlam becomes Secretary of State
6 July	Third crisis over Drumcree parade
10 July	Orange Order announces withdrawal of potentially contentious parades
20 July	IRA restores ceasefire

1998

10 April	Good Friday Agreement signed
2 May	Referenda endorse Good Friday Agreement
25 June	Elections to Northern Ireland Assembly
15 August	Bomb in Omagh kills 31 people

1

Settlement and civil war

Like every other diplomatic compromise in history, the 'Treaty between Great Britain and Ireland signed in London on December 6th, 1921' meant very different things to different people. Under its terms, Ireland was to become the Irish Free State, a Dominion within the British Empire, acknowledging the British monarch as sovereign. To the Irish delegation, led by the founder of Sinn Féin, Arthur Griffith, and the man who had masterminded the armed campaign for independence, Michael Collins, this represented the best deal which could be wrested from an empire which ruled much of the globe and which had just emerged victorious in a world war. If it conferred less than the Republic which had been proclaimed by Patrick Pearse in Dublin in 1916, it could still be represented as offering the means by which full independence might ultimately be secured. To others, the Treaty represented a grave dereliction from the republican enthusiasm which had carried Sinn Féin to its spectacular electoral victory in 1918 and then inspired the Irish Republican Army's (IRA) military struggle against the Crown. In particular, its terms were rejected by the most powerful figure in Irish politics, Eamon de Valera, the main survivor of the leaders of 1916 and President of Dáil Éireann, the body formed by the Sinn Féin MPs elected in 1918 as the legitimate government of the country. De Valera, who by choice had not been part of the Irish negotiating team in London, regarded Griffith and Collins as having failed to fulfil their instructions of referring the text of any agreement to

Dublin for ratification. To the British government of David Lloyd George, the Treaty was the means by which Irish nationalism could be reconciled to the empire, preserving the essential principles of imperial solidarity through the mechanisms of Dominion status and the monarchy. In addition, Britain retained the naval facilities of four ports, Queenstown (Cobh), Berehaven, Lough Swilly and Belfast, all regarded as basic to British security in the event of a renewed submarine campaign. For Lloyd George, too, the Treaty was the means by which Irish affairs could at last be taken off the British political agenda, an attitude maintained by his successors in London for over four decades.

Partition

Important as these considerations undoubtedly were, there was another dimension to the Treaty, partition. The partition of Ireland did not originate with the Treaty, but with Lloyd George's previous attempt at an Irish settlement, the Government of Ireland Act of 1920. This had tried to set up a parliament in Dublin for the 26 counties of Southern Ireland and another in Belfast for the six counties of Antrim, Armagh, Down, Fermanagh, Londonderry and Tyrone, to be termed Northern Ireland. 'Southern Ireland' failed to materialise in the face of Sinn Féin's contemptuous dismissal, but for the Ulster Unionists Northern Ireland represented their best hope of escaping from an all-Ireland parliament in Dublin. With Sir James Craig as Prime Minister, they seized on it with enthusiasm, celebrating the inauguration of their new parliament by King George V on 22 June 1921. But not everyone rejoiced. Their revered leader in the pre-war struggle against Home Rule, the Dubliner Sir Edward Carson, opposed partition and retired from political life. In this he was representing the bitter sense of betrayal felt by the unionist minorities elsewhere in Ireland, most notably in Dublin, Wicklow, Cork and the three Ulster counties of Cavan, Monaghan and Donegal. Their fears were by no means groundless. If the massacre of fourteen Protestants in Co. Cork in April 1922 was the exception, there was significant harassment of loyalists and their institutions. It is estimated that by the mid-1920s the Protestant population of the Free State had fallen by one-third. Seventy years later, the fate of their co-religionists in the south was still being cited by some northern Protestants as a reason for their unwillingness to compromise.

More significant for the future of Irish affairs was the sense of isolation felt by the nationalists of Northern Ireland. Two counties, Fermanagh and Tyrone, had clear nationalist majorities, as did its second city Londonderry, or Derry as nationalists preferred to call it. Substantial local nationalist majorities were also concentrated in south Armagh, south Down, the Glens of Antrim and the Falls district of Belfast. Overall, Northern Ireland had a Catholic nationalist minority of some 34 per cent, too large to be assimilated into the dominant Protestant unionist ethos of the new entity, or, ultimately, to be ignored. Northern Ireland as a continuing part of the British state ran so counter to the nationalist orthodoxy of a united Irish Republic that Griffith and Collins had been instructed in 1921 to break off negotiations on the issue of partition. In fact, Sinn Féin leaders acknowledged that some accommodation with northern Protestants was unavoidable and were willing to accept a Belfast parliament, though one subject to Dublin rather than London. But the Treaty allowed the Northern Ireland parliament to vote itself out of Dublin jurisdiction, thus cementing the 1920 partition. Griffith and Collins agreed to this on the basis of a Boundary Commission, which, they were led to believe, would give Tyrone, Fermanagh, Derry city, south Armagh and south Down to the Free State, thus rendering Northern Ireland economically unviable. They were deceived, for Lloyd George privately told his ministers that the Commission would probably lead to territory being added to Northern Ireland. Even without this knowledge, northern nationalists were incensed by their exclusion from a Dublin parliament and dismayed at their prospects under a unionist-dominated administration in Belfast.

The civil war and the consolidation of Northern Ireland

Between them, the Government of Ireland Act and the Treaty were the means by which the British government reached a settlement with the two main political forces which had emerged in Ireland, Sinn Féin and the Ulster Unionists, but events in Dublin and Belfast quickly exposed the fragility of the new structures. Griffith had scarcely arrived back in Dublin when he learned that de Valera would oppose what had been agreed. The nature and extent of that opposition was soon revealed in the Dáil debates on the Treaty which began on 14 December 1921 and lasted until 7 January 1922.

3

The essence of de Valera's position was that the Dominion status formula still left Ireland open to excessive British influence; he had long felt that the comparative independence enjoyed by countries such as South Africa and Canada was largely the result of their distance from Westminster. His preferred formula was 'external association' with the empire. Despite lobbying from northern nationalists, he did not propose to alter the sections of the Treaty dealing with Northern Ireland, but he did want to re-negotiate the nature of the imperial relationship. For their part, Griffith and Collins defended their agreement as realistic and principled, ridding Ireland of the reality of British power and opening the way to full national independence. In view of its later significance, there was curiously little debate on partition, though some speakers, including Monaghan's Sean MacEntee, warned that the practical result of the Treaty would be the inexorable growth of two Irelands. With convictions passionately held on all sides, it was not surprising that when the vote on the Treaty came on 7 January it was only by the narrow margin of 64 votes to 57 that Griffith and Collins held the day. When de Valera resigned as President and led his supporters from the Dáil, it was clear that the republican consensus had fractured.

The way was certainly open for Griffith, now President of the Dáil, and Collins, Chairman of the Provisional Government, to put in hand the new structures. Their moment in history came on 16 January 1922 when the new ministers entered Dublin Castle, long the seat and symbol of British rule. Despite de Valera's secession, the Provisional Government was not without assets. Among the population at large, there was greater support for the Treaty than the slim majority in the Dáil suggested. On the military side, Collins was supported by his old power base, the Irish Republican Brotherhood, and by key figures in the IRA, including its Chief of Staff, Richard Mulcahy, and his deputy, Eoin O'Duffy. Collins's key task was to convince other republicans that they should at least acquiesce in the new state, and certainly not take up arms against it. Initially at least, it seemed that no one was rushing into open confrontation. When the Sinn Féin Ard Fheis, or national convention, met on 21 February 1922, it was agreed that there should be no immediate vote on the Treaty and that elections would be postponed for three months. But it was an illusion, for there were elements in the IRA which were unwavering in their opposition to what they regarded as a betrayal of the Republic. Chief among them was Cathal Brugha, Minister of Defence in the campaign for independence,

4

who had long resented Collins and who had bitterly denounced him in the Dáil debates. Supporting de Valera and Brugha were a number of respected IRA veterans, including Ernie O'Malley, a Cork divisional commander who has left the best literary accounts of these events, Liam Mellows and Rory O'Connor. On 14 April 1922, O'Connor threw down his challenge to the Provisional Government by seizing the Four Courts and other buildings in the centre of Dublin; it was a clear echo of what Pearse and his men had done in 1916 but it raised the very different spectre of Irishmen firing on their former comrades.

Meanwhile, violence of another sort was being played out north of the border. Although there had been serious sectarian rioting in Belfast and other areas in 1920 and 1921, initially at least the Treaty seemed to hold out the prospect of the easing of tension. As far as James Craig was concerned, there was no reason why Northern Ireland should not reach a working arrangement with the Provisional Government on such essential all-Ireland services as the railways. At a meeting with Collins on 24 January 1922, he assured the southern leader that he would erect no barriers to an eventual united Ireland. For his part, Collins was acutely aware of the vulnerable position of the northern nationalists. But it proved to be a false start. In early February, the IRA seized a number of unionists from Fermanagh and Tyrone, including the 80-year-old Grand Master of the Orange Order in Tyrone, and held them hostage. This was in retaliation for the arrest of a group of armed men from Monaghan who were ostensibly travelling to a football match in Derry. The immediate crisis was defused when the groups were exchanged but it proved to be the start of some of the worst violence yet seen.

By March 1922, Belfast seemed in the grip of almost uncontrollable violence, with 61 deaths in the city, as well as numerous clashes and armed incidents in country areas. Faced with a near breakdown of civil order, Craig's government looked to its defences. Already available was the Ulster Special Constabulary (USC) which had been formed, at the suggestion of the British government, in November 1920. Partly recruited from Protestant vigilante groups which had been emerging across the six counties in response to the IRA, this provided the northern government with 1,600 full-time A Specials and 16,000 part-time B Specials, but did not constitute a proper police force, especially as the Royal Irish Constabulary (RIC) was due to hold its final parade in Dublin on 4 April. Craig turned for advice to one of the empire's leading soldiers, Field

Marshal Sir Henry Wilson, recently Chief of the Imperial General Staff and now Unionist MP for North Down. Wilson's recommendations, together with those of a committee which had been examining security needs, resulted in the formation of the Royal Ulster Constabulary, an armed force of 3,000, one-third of whose membership was to be reserved for Catholics. Its initial recruits were to be drawn from members of the A Special Constabulary and the Royal Irish Constabulary. In essence, this brought into being the policing structure which remained in place until the Hunt Committee recommendations of 1969. The RUC was distinctive from other police forces in the United Kingdom, and indeed from the new Gárda Síochána which replaced the RIC in the Free State, in having an overt security role in support of the state. While its record in challenging the IRA ensured the active support of the unionist community, a gulf existed between its members and nationalists which the passage of time did not erode. Certainly, the force never came near its objective of one-third Catholic membership. The part-time USC, or the B Specials as its members continued to be popularly known, was regarded by Catholics as little other than an armed militia at the service of unionist interests. For Protestants, particularly in isolated rural areas, its members were a guarantee of security.

Craig's government also turned its attention to the legislative framework. The Civil Authorities (Special Powers) Act, which came into force on 7 April 1922, gave his Minister of Home Affairs widespread powers, including that of detention without trial. However justified this legislation might have been by the mayhem going on in Belfast, it was a measure which clearly devolved great responsibility on the minister in question. Richard Dawson Bates, who held the ministry from 1921 to 1943, was not the man to rise to the challenge. A former secretary to the Ulster Unionist Council, he never escaped from the conviction that Catholics were rebels, real or potential. Under his regime the Special Powers Act, as it was commonly known, had a legacy far beyond the immediate crisis of the spring of 1922. It cannot be denied that the crisis was real enough. By the end of May, 236 people had been killed in Belfast, including 73 Protestants, 147 Catholics and 11 members of the security forces. While savage fighting continued in many parts of Belfast, including the murder of W. J. Waddell, Unionist MP for Woodvale, even more dramatic events were unfolding along the newly established border. Almost certainly in an attempt to aid the embattled Catholic areas of Belfast, strong IRA units occupied the area in the west of Fermanagh known as the Pettigo–Belleek Triangle. On this occasion the government in London decided to meet the challenge to what had become the only land border of the United Kingdom by the deployment of an infantry brigade. On 22 June, violence spread to London when Sir Henry Wilson was assassinated in a freelance operation by the local IRA.

Wilson's death helped bring to a head the crisis in Dublin, for the British government now demanded that Collins take action against O'Connor's men in the Four Courts. Attempts by Collins and de Valera to find an acceptable compromise which would avert civil war had come to nothing. The real test of how the public at large regarded the Treaty, and the new political dispensation, came in the elections held in the Free State on 16 June. The message sent by the electorate was interesting. Of the 620,283 votes, 239,193 went to pro-Treaty candidates compared with 133,864 for candidates opposed to the Treaty. But 274,226 votes went to Labour, Farmers and Independent candidates, signalling that for a large section of the electorate it was time to move on to other issues. With the anti-Treaty supporters so clearly in the minority, the government had the confidence to act. On 28 June, reinforced by artillery supplied by the British, the Free State forces began their assault on the Four Courts garrison, which was forced to capitulate two days later. The civil war which had threatened since the Dáil vote on the Treaty had become reality. Like every other civil conflict it was to leave a bitter legacy.

Ireland had already lost much of its potential political elite. The old Parliamentary Party had disappeared in the 1918 election. A number of possible future leaders had died as a result of the 1916 Rising and the war of independence; nor should it be forgotten that 35,000 Irishmen of all political persuasions had died in the First World War. Now the civil war exacted a further toll. An early prominent victim was Cathal Brugha, who was killed on 5 July leading the anti-Treaty forces in O'Connell Street. Rory O'Connor and Liam Mellows, captured at the Four Courts, were executed on 8 December, with a number of their comrades. In April 1923, Liam Lynch, who had become Chief of Staff of the anti-Treaty forces, was mortally wounded in an ambush. But the Provisional Government suffered two even more grievous losses. On 12 August 1922, Arthur Griffith, depressed and wounded by the turn of events since he had returned with the Treaty, died of a cerebral haemorrhage. Just ten days later, on 22 August, Michael Collins was shot dead in an ambush in Co. Cork. Still only 31 at the time of his death, Collins was fated to become the 'lost leader' of Irish politics. His potential unrealised, he had revealed enough to make his death a tragedy for the new state. Tragic, too, was the scale of casualties, which, by the time the civil war was brought to a halt in May 1923, perhaps numbered as many as 4,000.

2

Political and economic evolution: North and South

Out of this bloodletting two leaders of stature remained. Once again, Eamon de Valera proved to be the great survivor of republican politics. Never a military leader after his moment of glory in 1916, de Valera worked through the winter of 1922–1923 to secure an end to hostilities which would fall short of a republican surrender. But in May 1923 even he had to confront the reality of a Free State military victory. Emerging from hiding in August 1923, he was duly arrested. His imprisonment in Kilmainham and Arbour Hill prisons until July the following year enabled him to add a new dimension to his already impressive revolutionary credentials. De Valera was clearly building for a future when the republican movement, which he still considered the legitimate government of the country, would reclaim its inheritance. Events were soon to signal that this time might not be too far distant.

Collins's replacement as head of the Provisional Government, and then from December 1922 President of the Executive Council, was the veteran Sinn Féiner, W. T. Cosgrave. Cautious and conservative, Cosgrave proved to be an ideal conciliator for a country which needed reconciliation and construction after the violent struggles of the previous years. In this, he was ably sustained by two tough young disciples of Collins, Richard Mulcahy and Kevin O'Higgins, who had proved unrelenting in their opposition to the republicans in the civil war. In March 1923, Cosgrave consolidated the pro-Treaty forces in a new political party, Cumann na nGaedheal, but any hope that he could repeat the electoral success of Griffith and Collins the previous year was soon confounded. Seeking to capitalise on his victory in the civil war, Cosgrave called an election in August 1923. In an electorate enlarged by the admission of women over 21 to the franchise, Cosgrave increased his popular vote, but only to see a large increase in the Sinn Féin vote, aided by a decline in the support for Labour. Had it not been for Sinn Féin's refusal to take the oath of allegiance to King George V, and hence to take their seats, Cosgrave would have found it hard to sustain his majority in the Dáil.

Even so, Cosgrave dominated the political agenda of the Free State for the first decade of its existence, overcoming a so-called 'army mutiny' in 1924 and the assassination of O'Higgins by the IRA three years later. Cosgrave inherited a country which, despite the heady idealism of the period since 1916, was profoundly conservative. Fundamental to that conservatism was the fact that Ireland was still an agrarian society, with farming accounting for over 50 per cent of paid employment. The Wyndham Land Act of 1903 had brought into focus a process by which the land of Ireland was progressively transferred from the Anglo-Irish landlord class to those who worked it. By the 1920s the creation of a prosperous farming class was well under way, in contrast to the bitter agrarian discontent of earlier decades. For Cumann na nGaedheal, and particularly its Minister of Agriculture, Patrick Hogan, the generation of agricultural incomes and prosperity held the key to economic progress. This meant nothing less than the reversal of the principle of protectionism which had long underpinned nationalist political thought. With the British markets taking some 98 per cent of Irish exports, the bulk of them agriculturally related, Hogan pursued a free trade policy, aimed at high-quality exports of butter, eggs and cattle to Great Britain. In this, he had some fair measure of success, sustaining in the process the important social class which provided his party with solid support.

The other great engine of conservatism was the Catholic church, to which some 93 per cent of the population belonged. While Protestants continued to be strongly represented in the business and commercial life of the Free State, their political power had entirely gone. Since the members of Cosgrave's government came in the main from the same classes in society as the clergy, it is not surprising that their social policy sought to sustain Catholic social teaching, especially on matters of sexual morality. An early example was the Censorship of Films Act of 1923, followed six years later by the Censorship of Publications Act, which sought to ban indecent works which included, in their day, books by such authors as Ernest Hemingway and Jean-Paul Sartre. The ethos of the new state was also fostered through the encouragement of the Irish language, both in the administration and in the educational system, where it became a compulsory subject in 1924. If the official push behind the Irish language showed a sensitivity by the Free State government that its members had settled for something less than the aspirations of Irish nationalism, so, too, did their attitude towards the empire. While Free State representatives played their part in the Imperial Conferences of the time, in concert with the South Africans and Canadians they hastened the process towards the Statute of Westminster of 1931 which freed Dominion parliaments from their theoretical subordination to London. In that sense, Cosgrave's government was working out the reality of Collins's conviction that the Treaty gave Ireland the means to achieve its full independence.

By that time, the days of Cumann na nGhaedheal in government were numbered and it fell instead to Collins's great rival to achieve what he had predicted. By 1926 de Valera had concluded that he would have to re-enter the political mainstream, even at the cost of some compromise. To do otherwise would simply leave the field open to his opponents. When he failed to convince his party's Ard Fheis that it should enter the Dáil provided the oath of allegiance were removed, he resigned from Sinn Féin to form a new republican party, Fianna Fáil, which was to dominate the political life of independent Ireland. The first fruits of de Valera's initiative came in the elections of June and September 1927, which saw the two main parties closely matched. In June, Fianna Fáil gained 45 seats to Cumann na nGhaedheal's 47; Sinn Féin was reduced to a rump of five, while the smaller parties did well. The way was now open for entry into the Dáil which de Valera and his colleagues effected by signing the book containing the oath while covering up the wording. The September election saw the small parties squeezed. Cosgrave increased his seats to 62, but with 57 Fianna Fáil had created a two-party system, opening the way to a change of government. The next election, held in February 1932 in the bleak economic aftermath of the Wall Street Crash, saw de Valera at last enter his political inheritance. Winning 72 seats, Fianna Fáil was the largest party, able to govern in coalition with Labour. This was the most decisive election in modern Irish history. Not only was the way open for de Valera to set in hand his vision of Ireland's future but it showed that the democratic system

11

could survive the bitterness of the civil war. It led some to wonder whether the civil war had been necessary at all.

While Cosgrave was addressing the problems of the Free State, north of the border Craig, too, had begun the complex matter of state building. He began energetically enough. Never entirely convinced of the good faith of the Lloyd George government, Craig spent the winter of 1920–1921 setting up a credible administration, the backbone of which was in place by the time of the inauguration of the new government in June. Some of his ministers, including his Minister of Education, the Marquess of Londonderry, were experienced political veterans and he had a respectable cadre of civil servants. Even so, the challenges facing the new Northern Ireland government were daunting, not least the political viability of the new entity. Some form of irredentism from Dublin was always a possibility, while Craig had seen enough of Lloyd George's tactics to make him wary of London politicians. The very nature of the constitutional arrangement, a home rule parliament in Belfast, clearly indicated that what unionists liked to call the Imperial Parliament wished to keep them at arm's length.

These fears found their focus in the work of the Boundary Commission of 1924–1925, the mechanism which Griffith and Collins hoped, and Craig feared, would so truncate Northern Ireland as to leave it unviable. Under the chairmanship of the South African jurist, Richard Feetham, with the veteran newspaper editor, J. R. Fisher, and Eoin MacNeill, the scholar and politician, representing respectively the Belfast and Dublin governments, the Commission spent almost a year receiving evidence from interested parties along the border. When on 7 November 1925 its outline proposals were leaked to the conservative London newspaper, the *Morning Post*, it was clear that nationalist hopes were to be confounded. Working from the premise that his charge was to delineate a boundary rather than reconstitute the two states, Feetham rejected the wholesale transfer of Fermanagh and Tyrone to the Free State. A different argument was used for Newry, which was 74.6 per cent nationalist, and Derry City, which was 56.2 per cent nationalist. Here Feetham referred to an article in the Treaty which insisted that the wishes of the inhabitants had to be compatible with economic and geographical considerations. Since the principal industries of Newry and Londonderry were tied in with the Northern Ireland economy, he argued that they could not be transferred to the Free State.

The Commission's proposals, therefore, were that small areas with clear nationalist majorities, as around Crossmaglen (Co. Armagh), would go to the Free State, but that certain unionist enclaves, notably in east Donegal, would be transferred to Northern Ireland. These leaked proposals created such a stir in political circles that the work of the Commission was brought to an end. Unionism's strategy of 'what we have, we hold' seemed vindicated but whether a more homogeneously Protestant entity would be more stable in the long run was not much debated; most unionists felt they had surrendered enough with Cavan, Monaghan and Donegal and were disinclined to part with two more counties, still less the historic city of Londonderry whose siege in 1688–1689 had become the metaphor for the Protestant tradition of defiance. The composition and activities of Londonderry Corporation, in which a minority of unionist voters elected a majority of the members, became a particular source of nationalist grievance.

Craig's government might have overcome the most serious threat to its viability, but others remained. The devolutionary measures embodied in the 1920 Government of Ireland Act were deficient in two key areas. The first was revenue, without which no government can really claim to exert authority. The bulk of Northern Ireland's finance, some 90 per cent, derived from overall United Kingdom sources of revenue, such as income tax, over which the Belfast government had no control. Out of Northern Ireland's allocation was taken the 'imperial contribution', to pay its share of such United Kingdom services as defence. The nature of these sums resulted in bitter disputes between the Ministry of Finance and the Treasury in London. The only financial devices at Belfast's disposal were motor vehicle and death duties, hardly the basis of a credible financial policy. As the economic problems of the inter-war period increased, Craig's government had scant resources with which to tackle them. Thus the Northern Ireland administration effectively lacked the basis of any viable government, control over revenue. In that sense, it was hardly a government at all.

These financial problems were largely shielded from the population but the other legacy of the 1920 Act – the nature of the democratic structure – was not. The governmental structure, based on a House of Commons, was modelled on Westminster. But the Westminster system worked on the principle that the shifting fortunes of electoral fashion would result in periodic changes of government. In Northern

Ireland, where party allegiance was largely determined by religious denomination, this principle could not apply, or at least not as long as unionism could maintain its solidarity within a single party. The result was the monopoly of government by the Unionist Party. It is a truism of politics that a political party which is not subject to the periodic discipline of the electorate will stagnate. The long premiership of Craig between 1921 and his death in office in 1940 showed just such symptoms. The opposition fared no better. Most Nationalist MPs did not take their seats until 1928, but even then more with a view to the airing of grievances than with the intention of making a constructive contribution to political life. Their negativity, while understandable, did little to encourage unionists to make moves in their direction.

What Craig feared more than nationalism was a fracturing of unionism, either through the growth of a populist unionism or through the appeal of the Labour Party to the Protestant working class. Electoral results in 1918 and 1920 seemed to confirm the possibility of the latter. The Ulster Unionist Labour Association sought to counter the threat. Three of its members were elected in predominantly working-class Protestant Belfast constituencies in 1921, Oldpark, Pottinger and St Anne's, but in the 1925 election these three seats were gained by actual Labour candidates. The same election also confirmed the potential threat from the populist right, with four independent unionists taking seats. Faced with this, in 1929 Craig abolished proportional representation in favour of single member constituencies, with the result that political representation became intractably encased in the Unionist/Nationalist diarchy, even though an occasional maverick, such as the long-serving independent unionist Tommy Henderson in the Shankill, proved the exception. Even before 1914 unionism had been an uneasy alliance of class interests, with potential divisions between town and country, between landlord and tenant, or between Presbyterian and Church of Ireland.

On each side, particular institutions served to reinforce the sectarian divide. The most prominent of these in the unionist community was the Loyal Orange Institution, with which were linked, in the public mind at least, the Royal Black Institution and the Apprentice Boys of Derry Association. The Orange Order, which dated back to 1795, had been in many respects the guiding force behind the formation of Ulster Unionism in the late nineteenth century. As a result, the Order was formally represented in the key decision-making bodies in the Unionist Party. With few exceptions, unionist MPs were Orangemen,

Craig himself being County Grand Master of Down. The public face of the Orange Order seemed to define Northern Ireland, particularly so when the principal Orange celebration, the Twelfth of July, became a public holiday. The summer marches commemorating the Battle of the Boyne and the Relief of Derry were celebrated by Protestants as the definition of their identity, while being resented by Catholics as unionist triumphalism. The Catholic community had no real equivalent, the Ancient Order of Hibernians being a pale reflection of the Orange Order, with no access to the levers of political power. Instead, Catholics found their outlets in their church and through the playing of Gaelic sports.

If the two sides agreed on anything, it was education. The first Minister of Education was the Marquess of Londonderry, for whom education was more than the reinforcement of community identity. His purpose was the creation of a system of primary schools which would draw their pupils from both communities and avoid religious instruction. This brought on his head such a storm of wrath from both the Catholic hierarchy and the Protestant clergy, supported by the Orange Order, that Craig had to back down. The churches' role in education, except at university, remained, and children in Northern Ireland were educated within the comfortable embrace of their own tradition. Symptomatic of the depth of division in society was the way in which the commemoration of the recent war came to be the virtual monopoly of the unionist community. The legacy of the Home Rulers who had fought in the 16th (Irish) Division was an uncomfortable one for nationalists and republicans who preferred to honour the sacrifice of the men of 1916 and the war of independence. But for unionists the heroism of the 36th (Ulster) Division at the Battle of the Somme in 1916 had been the gauge of their loyalty to the Union. In the course of the 1920s Armistice parades and services took on the character of events which served to give legitimacy to the new polity of Northern Ireland. The poppy became a political statement as well as an emblem of commemoration.

Like every other government in the western world, Craig's had to confront the economic and social results of the post-war depression which devastated the industries on which Ulster's prosperity had been built. By the 1920s, linen was no longer much in fashion, and the industry, with its large female labour force, had to struggle on a low-wage basis. Shipbuilding throughout the United Kingdom found the post-war period hard. The Derry shipyard closed as early as 1924. The two large Belfast yards, the city's main employers of

15

skilled workers, Harland and Wolff and Workman Clark, survived the 1920s only to be hit by the great recession which followed the 1929 Wall Street Crash. The latter yard closed in 1935, while Harland and Wolff barely survived. Craig's ageing and socially conservative government had few resources with which to meet a situation in which over a quarter of the workforce became unemployed. The frustrations of the latter spilled over in October 1932 when disturbances in both Protestant and Catholic working-class areas of Belfast forced the government into an increase in unemployment relief. It was a brief moment of working-class unity, since, faced with the economic blizzard, there was an instinctive move on the part of each community to rally behind its own familiar banners. For the Protestant community this was reinforced by de Valera's 1932 electoral victory which promised a return to confrontation with Dublin.

3

From de Valera to the Republic

Eamon de Valera was the most durable, and arguably the most influential, Irish politician of the century. From the time he led his men into Boland's Mill in 1916 to his death in office as President in 1975 he was at the forefront of political life and controversy. He was never an easy man to categorise. Born in 1882 in New York to an Irish immigrant mother and a Spanish immigrant father, he came to Ireland as a young child. By 1916 he was both an officer in the Irish Volunteers and a dedicated republican. His record as the leading survivor of the Easter Rising and the skill with which he captured and then led Sinn Féin marked him out as a future leader. A man of unbending principle, he possessed a talent for political tactics which many came to see as at best contradictory. As a leader of independent Ireland he resembles other European statesmen, including Engelbert Dollfuss in Austria or Eduard Benes in Czechoslovakia, who tried to sustain the integrity of their new countries. Unlike them, he succeeded, though Neville Chamberlain's Britain was a very different animal to Adolf Hitler's Germany or Josef Stalin's Russia. His revolutionary instincts were political and constitutional rather than social or economic. Economics he barely understood, seeing Ireland as an agrarian society rather than one which needed to respond to the forces of industrialisation. His social views were soundly based on Catholic teaching. His two great aims, the rebirth of the Irish language and the ending of partition, ultimately eluded him; indeed, his critics have argued that he had no clear idea how to achieve them. But for

17

all that his passion for Ireland and its integrity are not in question and his place as one of the defining statesmen in the country's history is assured.

De Valera's victory in February 1932 can be seen as a fundamental test of the democratic structure of the Free State, since it saw power pass to the losing side in the bitter civil war which had been fought 10 years before. This is not to say that there were not bitter resentments and clashes between the IRA and the Army Comrades Association (ACA), which represented the veterans of the victorious Free State forces. In 1933, the ACA under Eoin O'Duffy took on some of the characteristics of extreme right-wing forces elsewhere in Europe. Terming itself the National Guard, it adopted the fascist salute and the uniform of the Blueshirts, the term by which it became popularly known. Despite such surface similarities with the Italian Blackshirts or Hitler's Brownshirts, Ireland did not produce a significant move towards fascism. In that respect, if in no other, it resembled Britain. The National Guard echoes Dollfuss's Catholic Austro-fascism rather than Hitler's virulently racist and expansionist National Socialism. Instead, the old Free State forces were forced into a realignment, not least by de Valera's second electoral victory in January 1933 which gave him an outright majority in the Dáil. Out of this defeat Cumann na nGaedheal and the National Guard formed Fine Gael, thus bringing into being the second of the two main political parties of independent Ireland.

Fianna Fáil's policy combined cultural, economic and political nationalism, and in particular was aimed at the dismantling of the 1921 settlement. In cultural terms, de Valera's vision of a Gaelic Ireland was pursued through the continued fostering of the Irish language. In economic policy the goal was greater self-sufficiency and industrial development through a tariff policy. Protectionism had long been a pillar of republicanism and its attractions were being more widely debated in the early 1930s in the aftermath of the Wall Street Crash. What brought Fianna Fáil's economic policy, and relations with Britain, into sharp focus was the question of land annuities. These were payments made by farmers under the Land Acts of the period 1891–1909 which had enabled them to purchase their farms from their landlords. Under financial arrangements made between the British and the Cosgrave governments in 1923 and 1926 the annuities were remitted to London. Not only were they resented in political terms; as some 18 per cent of government spending they were seen as a major barrier to economic progress. Since neither the 1923 nor the 1926 agreement had been ratified in the Dáil, de Valera considered himself free to address the issue at the earliest moment.

His first two major moves set the tone of the new politics. The first was the formal removal of the oath of allegiance to King George V. His second was to withhold payment of the land annuities. The British government's response was to impose a 20 per cent duty on imports from Ireland, which were, of course, chiefly agricultural. The Irish retaliated with duties on British exports of coal, cement, sugar, electrical machinery, and iron and steel, beginning what was termed the Economic War. As well as disrupting the established pattern of trade between the two islands, one unlooked-for consequence was to give more tangible form to the border between the two parts of Ireland through the erection of customs posts. In 1934 an agreement over coal and cattle, the most significant commodities for the two protagonists, took the sting out of the Economic War, but the vexed question of the annuities remained stubbornly in the background as profound constitutional changes were being prepared.

Next to the oath, the most obvious constitutional relic of the 1921 Treaty was the office of Governor-General. Its holder, James MacNeill, behaved with discretion towards the new government but by November 1932 he had been removed. His Fianna Fáil successor, Donal Ó Buachalla, ensured that the office ceased to have any meaning. There is no doubt that de Valera was working step by step towards the creation of a republic. In the spring of 1935 he began to prepare for what would be the cornerstone of the state, a constitution to replace the 1921 settlement, but in the course of this an unforeseen series of events in Britain intervened. The Abdication Crisis of November–December 1936, which saw Edward VIII abdicate in favour of his brother George VI, allowed de Valera to introduce two acts. The Constitutional Amendment Act effectively removed the monarch from the constitution, while the External Relations Act retained the symbolic role of the monarchy in foreign relations. By the end of 1936, then, de Valera had moved the Free State significantly in a republican direction.

The new constitution, approved by 685,105 votes to 526,945, came into effect on 29 December 1937. Under de Valera's guiding hand, it reflected republican aspirations and Catholic social teaching, tempered by a sense of pragmatism. The name Free State was replaced by Éire. In its preamble, the constitution remembered the 'heroic and unremitting struggle to regain the rightful independence of our Nation' and looked forward to seeing 'the unity of our country restored'. The latter aspiration was clearly embodied in Article 2, strongly resented by unionists, which stated that: 'The national territory consists of the whole island of Ireland, its islands and the territorial seas'. But Article 3 restricted the jurisdiction of the government to the 'area and extent of application as the laws of Saorstát Éireann' (that is, the twenty-six counties), a qualification which republicans saw as acquiescing in the reality of partition. While holding back from declaring a republic, Article 12 created the office of President (Uachtarán na hÉireann), with 'precedence over all other persons in the State'. Northern Protestants had their fears and suspicions confirmed in Article 44 whereby 'The State recognises the special position of the Holy Catholic Apostolic and Roman Church as the guardian of the Faith professed by the great majority of the citizens', even though the 'Church of Ireland, the Presbyterian Church in Ireland, the Methodist Church in Ireland, the Religious Society of Friends in Ireland, as well as the Jewish Congregations' were also recognised. Contemporary Catholic social teaching was reflected in the Articles on the family which forbade divorce and recognised 'that by her life within the home, woman gives to the State a support without which the common good cannot be achieved'. While these were not especially controversial at the time, they came increasingly under question from later generations of Irish women, especially when taken in conjunction with the 1935 ban on contraception.

Perhaps the constitution came into operation none too soon, for by 1938 the question had clearly arisen of Ireland's position in the increasingly likely prospect of war between the British Empire and Hitler's Germany. This set the context of negotiations between de Valera and the British prime minister, Neville Chamberlain, in the spring of 1938. The agreements which they reached on 25 April settled the land annuities question through an Irish payment of £10 million. More important was the removal of yet another pillar of the 1921 Treaty, through Britain's evacuation of the three southern treaty ports. This move was bitterly assailed by Chamberlain's leading domestic critic, Winston Churchill, one of those who had negotiated the 1921 settlement. For Churchill, the British government had surrendered the 'sentinel towers' of the western approaches which had been so vital to survival in the previous war. For Chamberlain, it was more important to have a friendly Ireland than to insist on Britain's rights to the ports. Both men were right, but events were to decide that Churchill's would be the dominant voice. For de Valera, the return of the ports was almost certainly vital to his chosen policy of neutrality in the event of a European conflict.

In systematically unpicking the Treaty, de Valera was consciously distancing Éire from the British imperial system. It was not lost on northern unionists that in so doing he was also sharpening the differences between the two jurisdictions in Ireland, at a time when sectarian tensions in Northern Ireland showed few signs of diminishing. The main reason for this was the devastating effect of the Great Depression on employment and living standards. Protestant sentiments were further heightened by the sense of Catholic pride over the International Eucharistic Congress in Dublin in the summer of 1932, in honour of which Catholic areas of northern towns and cities were decorated much in the manner of Protestant areas for the Twelfth of July. Unionists had their moment in November 1932 when the Prince of Wales opened the grandiose building for the Northern Ireland Parliament at Stormont, an event which offered nothing to nationalist sentiment. These events set the conditions for such appeals as that of the Fermanagh unionist MP and landowner, Sir Basil Brooke, for loyalists 'to employ Protestant lads and lassies', and Craig's declaration 'that we are a Protestant Parliament and a Protestant State'. Further down the social scale were the activities of the Ulster Protestant League which sought to assert the rights of Protestant workers against 'disloyal' Catholics. These sentiments went further than mere rhetoric. Sectarian trouble began in Belfast in 1934 and noticeably increased the following year, heightened by loyalist celebrations of King George V's Jubilee, so much so that a ban on parades was imposed which would have included the Twelfth of July demonstrations. Such was the furious response of the Orange Institution that the ban was lifted. As the annual Belfast demonstration neared its end, serious rioting broke out in the north of the city which lasted for days, leaving 13 dead, some 300 homeless, and considerable destruction of property. Intense though it was in the summer of 1935, the open sectarian tension was not sustained and proved to be the last major outbreak for the next three decades.

The Second World War and its aftermath

The 1930s may be summed up as deepening the partition of Ireland, economically and constitutionally. What confirmed this was the declaration of hostilities between the United Kingdom and Germany on 3 September 1939. Neither government in Ireland had prepared adequately for this, though because of its involvement in hostilities Craig's was the more culpable. Simply put, the war marked a clear distinction between Northern Ireland, which was involved in the war as an integral part of the United Kingdom, and Éire, which immediately proclaimed a policy of neutrality. As Britain declared war, de Valera's government passed the Emergency Powers Act, giving the events of the next six years the title of 'The Emergency'. De Valera really had little alternative. With a regular army of 7,000, almost totally lacking the accoutrements of modern warfare, his country was effectively defenceless. The only realistic hope of avoiding the fate of small countries such as Denmark, Norway, Holland and Belgium was a British victory. But any active involvement on Britain's side was precluded by partition and, despite a brief flirtation with the idea in 1940, there was never any serious prospect of the British government interfering with the status of Northern Ireland in wartime. Given Éire's ultimate reliance on the British armed forces and economy, there was never any doubt which way government policy would tilt. Within the limits of neutrality, assistance was given to the British and Allied side. The most public display of this was the despatch of Éire fire brigades to Belfast to assist with the aftermath of the air raids in the spring of 1941. There was extensive cooperation between the Irish and British intelligence services, not least in implementing de Valera's hard-line stance against an attempted IRA campaign in Britain. While standing firm against British pleas to be allowed the use of the former treaty ports, de Valera did permit flying boats from bases on Lough Erne to overfly Éire territory, thus avoiding long flights around Malin Head. No impediment was put in the way of recruitment, so that by 1945 some 43,000 Éire citizens had served in the British armed forces. On 31 May 1941, Dubliners experienced something of the reality of war when German bombers attacked the north of the city, killing 23. It was unclear whether this was the result of aircraft flying off course or a sharp warning to the Éire government which had recently sent help to Belfast. None of this was to earn de Valera much gratitude from Britain or its American ally. Churchill, in particular, bitterly resented his inability to use the treaty ports at a time when Britain's survival depended on winning the Battle of the Atlantic.

Despite Craig's assurance to the British people in February 1940 that 'We are the King's Men and we shall be with you to the end', in fact his somnolent government had left Northern Ireland almost totally unprepared for the conflict. In part this reflected the view that Belfast was too remote and uninteresting a target to attract the attention of the Luftwaffe. Hence, when the attacks did come in 1941 only some 25 per cent of Belfast's population were protected by air raid shelters. But it was also symptomatic of a somewhat semi-detached view of the war effort, at least in its early stages. What most obviously set Northern Ireland apart from the rest of the United Kingdom was that conscription did not apply, nor could it given the divided sentiments of the population. Enlistment remained stubbornly low for most of the war, some 38,000 overall. This was to some extent disguised by the extraordinary proportion of senior army commanders of Ulster origin: Field Marshals Alanbrooke, Alexander, Auchinleck, Dill and Montgomery.

Belfast was brought fully into the war through the large scale air attacks of 15–16 April and 4–5 May 1941. Some 900 people were killed in the first and 191 in the second, and half of Belfast's houses were destroyed or damaged. Perhaps as many as 100,000 took refuge in the countryside. Although morale was badly hit, nothing identified Northern Ireland so closely with the experiences of London, Coventry, Clydebank, Plymouth and other British cities as the blitz. Northern Ireland's main contributions to the Allied war effort were economic, and, above all, strategic. Although there were constant complaints about the low productivity of the workforce, Northern Ireland factories made a significant contribution to British war production. Harland and Wolff built three aircraft carriers and specialised in the construction of corvettes, so essential for convoy protection. Repair facilities at Belfast and Derry serviced over 3,000 vessels. The aircraft factories of Short and Harland, which had relocated from England in 1936, completed 1,200 Stirling bombers and 125 Sunderland flying boats. Mackie's Foundry produced 75 million shells and the Derry shirt factories were fully employed making uniforms.

Above all, Northern Ireland found itself able to contribute substantially to the Allied war effort through its strategic position, especially in relation to the Battle of the Atlantic. Churchill had been right in seeing the loss of Cobh and Berehaven (both in Co. Cork) as setting a major problem for convoy protection, the practical effect of which was to force all convoys through the North Channel to the Clyde and the Mersey, no longer protected by the Lough Swilly base (in Co. Donegal). Here Belfast Lough and, more especially the port of Londonderry and the Foyle estuary, proved invaluable, the latter extending the range of escort vessels by 100 miles. Derry rapidly built up into a major focus of naval activity, with as many as 120 escort vessels of the Royal Navy, the Royal Canadian Navy and United States Navy based there. With the shirt factories also fully employed, the city was for a time pulled out of the depression which had affected it deeply before the war. It was particularly appropriate that the bulk of the German U-boat fleet surrendered at Lisahally on the Foyle. Finally, Northern Ireland was used as one of the main assembly and training areas for the United States army in preparation for the invasion of Europe.

All of this meant that when victory came in May 1945 Northern Ireland had secured a claim on Britain which Éire, her unobstrusive cooperation notwithstanding, had not. Nor was this helped by de Valera's call on the German ambassador to convey his condolences on the death of Hitler. While diplomatically punctilious, given what the Red Army had recently uncovered at Auschwitz-Birkenau and the British at Belsen the wisdom of the call may be doubted. This was reflected, perhaps, in the bitterness with which Churchill attacked de Valera in his victory speech, broadcast to the world on 13 May. The British leader's rancour over the treaty ports boiled over: 'had it not been for the loyalty and friendship of Northern Ireland we should have been forced to come to close quarters with Mr. de Valera or perish forever from the earth'. His final sting was that 'we left the de Valera government to frolic with the Germans and later with the Japanese representatives to their heart's content'. Such a public rebuke could not go answered, and de Valera retorted in a broadcast three days later. The substance of his reply was that Britain's necessity could not be elevated into a moral code and that it was 'hard for the strong to be just to the weak'. No one could deny that the end of the war had left sour relations between Dublin and London, and these were not to change significantly when Churchill was replaced a few weeks later by the Labour government of his war-time partner, Clement Attlee.

The immediate post-war years were to have significant consequences for Ireland, though more particularly for the north. Because of the long-standing link between the Unionists and British Conservatives, and also because of the large Catholic vote for the Labour Party in areas like Clydeside and Merseyside, Attlee's government was assumed to have an instinctive sympathy towards the nationalist case. In fact, during the period of the post-war Labour government Northern Ireland became more closely bound in with the British system than it had ever been. At the same time, Éire was going through

24

the process of making its final breach with Britain and the Common-wealth. In July 1946, a new party, Clann na Poblachta, was formed under the leadership of a man with the most sea-green republican credentials, Sean MacBride. Not only was MacBride a former IRA Chief of Staff, but his father, John MacBride, was among the executed leaders of 1916, and his mother was Maud Gonne, one of the most vibrant nationalists of her day. Under MacBride, Clann na Poblachta threatened to cut into Fianna Fáil's natural constituency, and also raised the spectre of another split within republicanism. Somewhat hastily, de Valera called an election for February 1948 in the hope of choking off this unwelcome rival. The even more unwelcome, and perhaps unlikely, result was a coalition government of Fine Gael, Clann na Poblachta, Labour, National Labour, and the farmers' party, Clann na Talmhán. The new leader was John A. Costello, with MacBride as Minister for External Affairs. In September 1948, while on a visit to Canada, Costello made the startling announcement that he was going to declare a republic. This about-turn in Fine Gael policy came into effect the following year, when the Republic of Ireland also left the commonwealth. Ireland's formal divorce from Britain was now complete but in the fast changing circumstances of the post-war world this proved a matter of diminishing significance. Britain herself was now a power of the second rank, dominated by her principal ally, the United States. The onset of the Cold War led to the formation of the North Atlantic Treaty Organisation (NATO) in 1949, but, here too, Ireland held aloof. The continuance of partition meant that the Republic would not contemplate entering into a formal alliance with Britain. Through this isolation from what had become the central pillar of western diplomacy, Ireland further forfeited sympathy in London, and also in Washington where membership of the alliance had become the acid test of loyalty in a polarised world.

Such isolation was naturally welcome to unionism. Craig had died in November 1940. His successor, John Andrews, was a makeweight who was overthrown by his party in 1943 in favour of Sir Basil Brooke, the Fermanagh landowner whose speeches on employment in the 1930s had been neither forgotten nor forgiven by nationalists. Brooke, whose premiership was to last 20 years, was not the man to soften Northern Ireland's sectarian divisions. Even so, Brooke was wise enough to realise that a Labour government committed to social reform offered possibilities both for cementing the union and for holding the affections of the Protestant working class. In this respect he saw more clearly than some of his colleagues who floated the idea of dominion status for Northern Ireland. Described as 'step by step', Brooke's government ensured that the welfare provisions of the Labour government with regard to national insurance, the health service and housing were implemented in Northern Ireland. This social reconstruction of Northern Ireland was made possible by a restructuring of the financial relationship between the Ministry of Finance in Belfast and the Treasury in London. Perhaps the most significant of these reforms was the Education Act of 1947 which extended to Northern Ireland the main features of the 1944 Butler Education Act. This imaginative measure transformed the educational prospects of thousands of children from modest backgrounds by opening up grammar school places, particularly expanding opportunities for young Catholics. Later critics might castigate the division between grammar and secondary schools but the practical effect of the Act was to permit large numbers to proceed to university education who hitherto could only have looked on from outside the gates. The social and political consequences of this were to prove immeasurable. Finally, Brooke successfully lobbied London to secure Northern Ireland's constitutional position in the light of the Republic's departure from the Commonwealth. The Ireland Act of June 1949 formally enacted that: 'Northern Ireland remains part of His Majesty's Dominions and of the United Kingdom and . . . that in no event will Northern Ireland or any part thereof cease to be part of His Majesty's Dominions and of the United Kingdom without the consent of the Parliament of Northern Ireland'.

By 1949 the two jurisdictions in Ireland were further apart than most of those who had presided over the partition of 1920–1922 had imagined, most obviously so in constitutional terms. Irish republicanism had achieved one of its main aspirations by breaking free from the British imperial system, albeit at a time when that system was in any case in a state of terminal decline. Its other hope, of ending partition, seemed more aspirational than ever. The policies of de Valera and Costello had simply confirmed northern Protestant attitudes. Unionism was never as secure, or as confident, as in the years immediately after 1949. Still formally linked with British Conservatism, it had secured a far-reaching guarantee from Labour. For the next twenty years both British political parties maintained the convention of not interfering with the internal workings of the devolved government in Stormont. But nothing was being done about the great sectarian fault line in Northern Ireland politics and society. For northern nationalists their place had yet to be decided.

4

Post-war Ireland

The Republic cut a somewhat isolated figure in the world of the 1950s. The major issues of the time, having as their focus the Cold War and the possibility of nuclear warfare, concerned the two conflicting alliance systems led by Washington and Moscow. With its strong anti-communism, Ireland was never going to be wooed by the latter, but in such a polarised world the United States was unimpressed by neutrality. Northern Ireland retained some strategic importance for the NATO alliance. NATO warships became a familiar sight on the Foyle, Derry had the anti-submarine training school HMS *Sea Eagle* and an American naval communications base, while long-range RAF aircraft continued to patrol the western approaches from the wartime airfield at Ballykelly. While the Republic did join the Council of Europe in 1949, this proved a toothless body. Like Britain, Ireland held aloof from the more concrete moves towards European cooperation and unity which were being pushed forward in the early 1950s by such far-sighted individuals as Jean Monnet and Robert Schumann. Ireland was not involved in the various stages through which six western European countries, France, Italy, Federal Germany, Belgium, the Netherlands and Luxembourg, created the European Economic Community in 1957 in the Treaty of Rome. Ireland only really entered international affairs through her membership of the United Nations in 1955, but although Irish people took a justified pride in the role of their diplomats and soldiers, especially in the Congolese crisis of the early 1960s, in reality the international body only operated on the margins of what was allowed by the two superpowers.

Post-war readjustments: North and South

Throughout the 1950s, the Republic's political debate focussed largely on domestic issues, with partition providing an accompanying counterpoint. What stirred most emotions was the not unworthy issue of public health. Throughout the period from 1922 the major problem in the area of public health was tuberculosis, especially in the poorer urban areas. Although the incidence of the disease in Ireland was no worse than in comparable societies, the creation of the welfare state and health service in Britain exerted pressure for reform. The fight against tuberculosis was nothing less than a personal crusade for Clann na Poblachta's young Minister of Health, Dr Noel Browne. He was a survivor of the disease, while his father, mother and sister had died of it. By 1950 Browne had increased the number of beds for tuberculosis patients from 3,500 to 5,500 and in the following year cases of the disease fell rapidly. At the same time as his successful campaign against tuberculosis, Browne was working on further health reforms which would take up proposals set out by his Fianna Fáil predecessors in their Health Act of 1947. The essence of the scheme Browne set out in 1950 was that medical services would be provided for mothers and for children up to the age of 16 without a means test. The 'Mother and Child' scheme, as it became known, attracted the hostility not only of a well-entrenched medical profession but of the Catholic hierarchy. What alarmed the bishops was the implied extension of state power to matters of education, including health education, which were the domain of the church. More especially, they protested that provisions for gynaecological care could be taken to include birth control and abortion, both directly contrary to church teaching. Despite Browne's assurance that in educating mothers and children in matters of health, nothing would be included 'of an objectionable nature', on 4 April 1951 the hierarchy announced that the scheme was against the church's social teaching. Two days later the government decided to abandon the scheme and on 11 April Browne's resignation, in effect dismissal, took place. As Ulster Unionists were quick to point out, the affair reflected the influence the Catholic hierarchy could have on politics when it chose to exert it. In 1951, Browne was in some respects an easy target. The Costello government was always a potentially unstable coalition and it seems that not all members were convinced by Browne's scheme, a view perhaps confirmed by the speed with which he was despatched.

The coalition government did not long survive the Mother and Child controversy. The election of June 1951 actually saw a substantial increase in the Fine Gael vote, gaining the party nine extra seats, but this availed them nothing in the face of an almost total collapse of their Clann na Poblachta allies who were almost eliminated losing eight of their ten seats. With the support of Independents, some of them supporters of Noel Browne, de Valera and Fianna Fáil returned to power. The de Valera government of 1951–1954 is not held to have been a success. Partly this was an inevitable consequence of de Valera's advancing years; he was, after all, twenty years older than in the great days of 1932. But it was also the result of the parlous state of the country's finances. In order to combat a serious balance of payments deficit the government pursued a policy of deflation through the raising of income tax and prices of basic staples such as bread and tea. The result was a stagnant economy. A second coalition government headed by Costello from 1954 to 1957 had no greater financial or economic success. This was reflected in the persistence of that particular Irish malaise, the migration of its young people, mostly to Britain. In these depressing circumstances, the 1957 election saw de Valera triumph once again, this time with an overall majority in the Dáil. Clann na Poblachta was reduced to a single seat and disappeared as a force in political life. The period 1948–1957, then, was one in which Fianna Fáil managed to confirm its position as the dominant political force. Fine Gael, while it could not be discounted, had only been able to govern as part of a broadly based coalition.

Now seventy-five and with failing eyesight, de Valera had, however reluctantly, to contemplate political mortality. In 1959 he resigned as Taoiseach. From 1959 until 1975 he served as president, becoming a semi-legendary link with the events of 1916 and the turbulent emergence of the state in 1919–1922. His successor as Taoiseach, Sean Lemass, was another 1916 veteran but differed from his old chief in one important respect; he had an interest in, and a feel for, economics. As the increasingly dominant voice in the government from the time of the 1957 election, Lemass opened the way for policies of economic expansionism which moved Ireland forward from the old Fianna Fáil orthodoxies. Since at least the late 1940s there had been those, notably in the civil service, who had questioned the economic sense of protectionism combined with a continuing over-dependency on the British market. The financial and economic doldrums of the 1950s seemed to confirm the force of their analysis. The most influential advocate of a new fiscal and economic direction was T. K. Whitaker, secretary to the Department of Finance from 1956. The coming together of Whitaker and Lemass proved fortuitous since between them they were poised to take the country in a new direction.

The fruits of the new thinking came in two documents published in 1958, *Economic Development* and the *Programme for Economic Expansion*. Inspired by Whitaker, these set the direction and tone of Lemass's economic policy. What was proposed was a reversal of Fianna Fáil's protectionist policies in favour of free trade. Foreign investment in the country was to be encouraged, while government spending was to be adjusted in favour of production rather than the infrastructure or social projects such as housing. Like Franklin Roosevelt's New Deal in the United States, these proposals offered people the prospect of moving forward from the economic and fiscal stagnation of the post-war years. Lemass was fortunate in that his initiatives coincided with the period when western Europe in general was reviving economically after the wartime dislocation. This was the period, after all, when their British neighbours were being reassured that 'They never had it so good', and Dr Ludwig Erhard was presiding over the West German 'Economic Miracle'. Though still overly dependent on the British market, Ireland was now much better placed to respond positively in terms of exporting and economic growth. By 1960, the Irish exporting position showed clear signs of dramatic growth, both in the traditional areas of farm produce and in manufacturing. The new openness was also seen in trade relations with Britain, though whether Ireland should have been looking to a sluggish and unresponsive British economy is open to question. Certainly, when Britain applied for Common Market membership in 1961 Ireland had little option but to join her; equally, the Irish application perished when President de Gaulle vetoed British membership in 1963. The Anglo-Irish Free Trade Agreement of 1965 was a logical extension of this process. The Agreement, which aimed at free trade between the two countries by 1975, in a sense restored the economic relationship which had existed under the Union. Its significance should be seen in terms of the freeing of trade throughout western Europe as reflected in the European Economic Community and the European Free Trade Area. That the policies pioneered by Whitaker and Lemass set the conditions for Ireland's economic progress in the 1960s cannot seriously be questioned. That progress could not insulate the country against the buffetings of the international economy, as evidenced by the effects of the international energy crisis of 1973–1974. It has also been criticised for failing adequately to stimulate indigenous Irish industry. But by 1973, when Ireland entered the EEC alongside Britain, the country's economy was unrecognisable compared with the drift and stagnation which had characterised its situation 20 years earlier. Ireland was ready to take its place in an increasingly vibrant European Community.

For northern unionists the years after 1949 seemed ones of stability and hoped-for social and economic progress. Any lingering fears for Northern Ireland's constitutional position within the United Kingdom had been removed by the Ireland Act, while inclusion in the British Welfare State had freed ordinary people from the fears of unemployment and ill-health which had haunted them before the war. The Twelfth of July processions mirrored this confidence. The Orange demonstrations of the time were powerful manifestations of unionism's seemingly invincible supremacy. Brethren were addressed by Northern Ireland cabinet ministers, senior churchmen and visiting Conservative MPs, while photographs confirm the well-filled ranks of lodges, especially in Belfast. In September 1962 Brooke combined his roles as Prime Minister and senior Orangeman when he presided over the Orange Order's parade and rally to commemorate the fiftieth anniversary of the signing of the Ulster Covenant. Interesting absentees on the occasion were the Orangemen of Donegal, Cavan and Monaghan who did not feel that their signatures in 1912 had gained them much. Otherwise, the occasion was a massive display of unionist pride and solidarity, one of the last as it happened.

The official view of Northern Ireland was portrayed in *The Ulster Guide*, published in 1947. Ulster, noted Brooke in his foreword, was known throughout the world for its majestic ships, its beautiful linen and the varied products of its many manufacturing industries. The Belfast depicted was that of the 'majestic edifice' of the Stormont parliament buildings, City Hall, the Ulster Museum, Queen's University, the Botanic Gardens, and Robinson and Cleaver's department store, as well as Harland and Wolff, Short Brothers' aircraft factory, Gallaher's Tobacco Factory, the York Street Linen Mills and 'the world's greatest ropeworks'. The photographs of the city of Londonderry told their own story: the Guildhall, the war memorial, and the familar icon of the Walker Pillar with the siege cannon on the walls. More than 30 factories were recorded, employing thousands in the production of shirts and collars. This was the Ulster of the Giant's Causeway, craftsmen at Belleek, cottages in the Sperrins, and the holiday resorts of Bangor, Portrush and Portstewart which attracted thousands from industrial Clydeside every summer. To say that this roseate view of Northern Ireland was partial is merely to state the obvious, but it is important to do so since it was a perception which coloured the attitudes of a generation of unionists and helps explain their angry and perplexed reactions when it was suddenly and violently challenged. For unionists this was a golden age when, they believed, Catholics contentedly watched the annual processions on the Twelfth of July and loyalist bandsmen lent their instruments to their nationalist counterparts.

Behind this image lay a sterner reality of industrial decline and political stagnation. Nowhere was the former more dramatically seen than in the linen industry which could not respond to the challenge of artificial fibres. With nearly 76,000 workers, mostly female, at the start of the 1950s, by the end of the decade the industry had all but collapsed. Employing 20,000 men, Harland and Wolff still dominated the industrial profile of Belfast. Throughout the 1950s the yard maintained a high level of construction as world trade revived after the war. It was a bubble fated to burst. In common with the rest of the British shipbuilding industry, Harland and Wolff failed to respond to the new methods of ship construction being developed in German, Swedish and Japanese yards. The Belfast yard had long been famous for its construction of passenger liners but by the late 1950s more people were crossing the Atlantic by air than by ship. In that sense the great liner *Canberra* was already an anachronism at the time of its launch in 1960. Harland and Wolff simply mirrored the problems of British shipbuilding which were to see the devastation of the industry on the Clyde, Tyne, Wear and Mersey. Parallel with these danger signals in the industrial sector, mechanisation in the countryside was reducing the need for farm labourers. In many respects the Northern Ireland economy was displaying in miniature the lacklustre performance of the United Kingdom economy in this period. But in such a relatively small society the impact of economic decline, most obviously in unemployment rates, was going to be more intense. Northern Ireland consistently displayed the highest levels of unemployment in the United Kingdom, in the cases of Derry, Strabane and Newry dramatically so.

During this period of unionist ascendancy the frustrations and aspirations of the nationalist minority were expressed in a variety of ways, none of them effective. In November 1945 a meeting of nationalists agreed to set up the Irish Anti-Partition League in an attempt to create a body which would embrace the various shades of nationalist opinion. Hopes of influencing the new Labour government in London proved illusory. Labour maintained the convention by which Westminster did not intervene in matters which had been transferred to the Northern Ireland parliament. Such was the degree of nationalist anger over the Ireland Act that in the February 1950 General Election the League ran candidates in Bootle, Coatbridge, Greenock and Glasgow Gorbals, without making any noticeable inroad into the well-established working-class Catholic support for the Labour Party. Much was hoped for from Sean MacBride's presence in the 1948 coalition government, but moves to give northern nationalists the right to attend the Dáil were blocked by Costello. During his period in opposition de Valera was vehement in his denunciations of partition, but once back in power in 1951 he, too, was determined that northern nationalists should not have access to the Dáil. Neither Costello nor de Valera, it seems, was anxious to see northerners involved in the politics of the south, a view shared by most members of the Dáil. When MacBride, now out of power, introduced a motion in July 1951 which would have given northern nationalists the right of audience in the Dáil, the measure was defeated by 82 votes to 42. Frustrated in both London and Dublin, nationalists had only two options left; to defend their position through attendance at Stormont or to turn to violence.

Whether or not to take their seats in the parliament of Northern Ireland had from the start been a vexed issue for nationalists. These tensions found their focus in the Stormont elections of October 1953, especially in the contest in the Foyle constituency which took in most of the nationalist electorate of Derry city. Paddy Maxwell, who had held the seat since 1937 on an abstentionist position, was challenged by a group of nationalists who believed in using Stormont as a vehicle for their grievances. Their champion was Eddie McAteer, who had already represented the Mid Londonderry constituency since 1945 and become Chairman of the Nationalist Party in 1953. Standing as a Nationalist, McAteer defeated Maxwell, Independent Nationalist, by 6,953 votes to 4,412. A dedicated constitutionalist, whose brother Hugh had been a senior IRA commander, McAteer's was to be the dominant voice of northern nationalism for the next 15 years. Under his hand the Nationalist Party ensured that the cause of Irish unity was kept alive and that the problems of the Catholic community were heard. As a party, however, it was really little more than a coalition of local interest groups and personalities. Its MPs and leaders, accountants, journalists, farmers, lawyers and merchants, were drawn from no broader a social base than its unionist opponents. This, combined with its Derry-based leadership and MPs from rural Catholic areas, meant that the party attracted virtually no support in working-class Catholic Belfast. No member of the Nationalist Party sat for a Belfast constituency after 1946.

McAteer's constitutionalism was also under challenge from republicanism. The first sign that the IRA might be planning a campaign came in June 1951 when its Derry unit secured a quantity of arms from HMS *Sea Eagle*. Then, in June 1954, a raid on Gough army barracks in Armagh secured 254 rifles, 30 sub-machine guns and nine machine guns. In the Westminster elections of May 1955 the strength of republican feeling was seemingly demonstrated when Sinn Féin candidates, both serving prisoners, narrowly defeated Unionists in the Mid Ulster and Fermanagh and South Tyrone constituencies. The actual IRA campaign began on the night of 11–12 December 1956 with attacks on a variety of targets in places as far apart as Magherafelt, Dungannon, Armagh, Derry city, Fermanagh and north Antrim. Although activity was at a high level well into 1957, the IRA never came close to its objectives of forcing a breakdown in the administration of Northern Ireland and establishing secure bases in nationalist areas. The security campaign was waged almost entirely by the RUC and the USC, securing in unionist eyes the pivotal position of these institutions. Both Belfast and Dublin governments used internment against IRA leaders and activists, thus confirming the jaundiced republican view of de Valera which dated back to his apparent compromise over the oath in 1927. But the IRA campaign really foundered on the rock of the indifference of the majority of the nationalist population inside Northern Ireland. Pressed hard by the security forces north and south of the border, in February 1962, the IRA announced the 'termination' of a campaign which by then had cost the lives of 12 people, six of its own and six members of the RUC.

By the time the IRA campaign collapsed, the unionist leadership had other concerns since the economic problems which had been building up through the 1950s threatened to become stark. In 1961, Harland and Wolff and Short Brothers announced large-scale job losses as a result of lack of orders. These were blows not just at Belfast but at the skilled Protestant working class which lay at the heart of unionism. Ever since the 1918 general election unionist leaders had worried about the potential defection of Protestant workers and the results of the 1958 Stormont election seemed to give substance to these fears. Labour MPs were elected from the Belfast constituencies of Victoria, Woodvale, Pottinger and Oldpark. The loss of Victoria in solidly Protestant east Belfast and of Woodvale at the head of the loyalist Shankill Road was particularly galling and worrying. In the 1962 election, while the Northern Ireland Labour Party failed to gain more seats, its vote increased by some 15 per cent. These unsettling economic and political developments lay behind the end of the 20-year premiership of Lord Brookeborough, as Brooke had become, in March 1963.

5

O'Neill and the rise of the civil rights campaign

Brooke's successor, Captain Terence O'Neill, also represented the established landowning elite within unionism, but there the resemblance with Brooke appeared to end. O'Neill was determined to move Northern Ireland forward on two fronts, by attracting economic investment and by modernising unionism. As Minister of Finance, he had been impressed by the economic measures being set in hand south of the border. In the course of the 1950s progress had been made in attracting artificial fibre companies to establish plants. Under O'Neill's Minister of Commerce, Brian Faulkner, European and American firms including Grundig, ICI and Goodyear invested in Northern Ireland. This sense of dynamism was further generated as Northern Ireland replicated that classic British device of the 1960s, the government report; these years saw the Matthew report on the Belfast region, the Benson report on the railways, the Wilson report on the economy and the Lockwood report on higher education. These were to have political ramifications rather different to their authors' intentions.

In political terms, O'Neill saw the threat to unionism as coming from the Northern Ireland Labour Party. Here, he had some success. The 1965 Stormont election saw Victoria regained for the Unionist Party by the articulate former television producer Roy Bradford, while the victory in Woodvale of the ex-docker and Chindit John McQuade strengthened the party's claim to be the authentic voice of the Protestant working class. What O'Neill did not foresee was that the challenge to his form of unionism would come from a very different direction. What triggered that attack was his policy of making gestures of accommodation towards the minority community. These were a matter of tone rather than substance, such as his visit to a Catholic convent school. More dramatic was his invitation to Seán Lemass to come to Stormont. Their meeting, on 14 January 1965, symbolised an intention to work towards a warmer relationship on the island. One interesting consequence was the decision made by the Nationalist Party the following month that they should assume the role of Official Opposition at Stormont, a move which, as McAteer well knew, was not without its dangers. For O'Neill the talks meant breaking a unionist taboo on meeting southern leaders while the territorial claim in the 1937 constitution remained in force, while for Lemass it implied a degree of recognition of the northern polity. But O'Neill's decision not to inform his cabinet in advance of the meeting betrayed a sense of uneasiness about unionist reactions. Although the election results the following October did not seem to bear out such fears, it was not long before stresses in the Protestant community began to show. O'Neill's background and personality did not really equip him to respond to the kind of populist challenge which developed. Although he was personally more affable than popular belief suggested, he did lack a common touch. He was a member of the Orange Order, and as Prime Minister joined the Apprentice Boys of Derry, but his role in these organisations never carried much conviction. In addition, he had powerful rivals within the party, not least his ablest minister, Brian Faulkner.

The danger signals began to appear in 1966. On 27 May, a young Catholic, John Scullion, was mortally wounded in a gun attack in Belfast. On 26 June, gunmen opened fire on four Catholic barmen in Malvern Street off the Shankill Road, killing one of them, Peter Ward. These attacks were the work of the recently formed Ulster Volunteer Force (UVF), based in the Shankill. Three men were imprisoned for the murder and the UVF was immediately banned by an embarrassed government. A different challenge to O'Neill was the rising evangelical Protestant clergyman, the Reverend Ian Paisley. Although in 1966 he seemed a distant threat to O'Neill, he was to prove the most durable unionist politician of them all. If O'Neill personified the aristocratic element within unionism, and Brian Faulkner the middle-class manufacturer, then Paisley was in direct line of descent from the dissenting Protestant traditions of the 1859 Revival and the fiery evangelist of the 1920s, W. P. Nicholson.

The son of an independent Baptist minister, his roots in Protestant fundamentalism ran deep. Integral to his deeply held beliefs was a rejection of the claims of the Catholic church, combined with a distrust of what he saw as the ecumenical tendencies of the established Protestant churches. In political terms this translated into a conviction that O'Neill and the unionist leadership were preparing to undermine the Protestant basis of Northern Ireland. In 1951, after a split among Presbyterians in Crossgar, Paisley founded the Free Presbyterian Church of Ulster. His real entry into politics came with the 1964 Westminster election when he materially helped James Kilfedder to win West Belfast for the Unionists. His protests over the public display of an Irish tricolour in the Republican candidate's headquarters in Divis Street prompted police action which resulted in serious rioting. An instinctive and emotive public speaker, Paisley was well placed to articulate the doubts felt by many Protestants over O'Neill's attempts at accommodation. When Lemass's successor, Jack Lynch, visited Stormont in December 1967, Paisley and his supporters were there to protest. 'Paisleyism', as it was termed, might still have seemed to be on the outer fringes of unionism, but its moment was soon to come, and to prove enduring over the next three decades. Political leaders would attempt to dismiss Ian Paisley at their peril.

O'Neill's policies, while feeding loyalist fears and causing unease in sections of his party, were too late and too little to head off the explosion of protest which surfaced in the Catholic community in 1968. Like most revolutions, for it was nothing less, this had long-standing and immediate causes. Underlying what happened was the widespread feeling among nationalists that they were marginalised in terms of the power structures of Northern Ireland, that Stormont was an impregnable unionist citadel, sustained by a civil service and police which were predominantly Protestant. Neither the constitutionalism of the Nationalist Party nor the violence of the IRA had done anything to alter this reality. Only once, in the case of the Wild Bird Act of 1931, did an opposition-sponsored bill pass into law. Governments in London and Dublin averted their eyes. By the middle of the 1960s, however, certain things were changing. As a result of the 1947 education reforms there was a growing grammar school and university educated section of the Catholic population, often of working-class origin, which was both disinclined to accept the status quo and dismissive of the tactics which had proved so ineffective over 40 years. Television was making protests elsewhere in the world instantly accessible. The black civil rights movement in the United States was an exemplar of non-violent protest. The Tet offensive in Vietnam, the 'Prague Spring' and the student riots in Paris took place in 1968. From 1964 Britain had once again a Labour government, this time led by Harold Wilson who represented a Merseyside constituency where Irish issues were understood. Inside the Labour Party the Campaign for Democracy in Ulster aired nationalists' grievances, while the election of Gerry Fitt as Republican Labour MP for West Belfast in 1966 ensured a strong, if lone, voice at Westminster.

By the mid-1960s, the nationalist sense of alienation had come to settle on certain issues, some of them associated with the policies of the O'Neill government. Hand in hand with an awareness of exclusion from the established power structures went experience of discrimination in jobs and housing. In fact, both Catholics and Protestants had long favoured 'their own' when it came to hiring labour, but the latter controlled more large firms and local authorities. Local authority jobs were a particularly sensitive issue. While nationalist Newry employed few Protestants, unionist authorities favoured their own supporters. Hence, out of 75 school bus drivers in Fermanagh seven were Catholics. Particularly in focus was the city of Londonderry and the nature and policies of its Corporation. With its substantial Catholic majority, Derry represented Northern Ireland in reverse, with the critical difference that in this case the minority was in control. From the middle of the 19th century, the city had a Catholic majority. But since nowhere evoked the traditions of the Ulster Protestant community so powerfully, unionism was determined not to let go its hold. 'No Surrender!', the watchword of the siege of 1688–1689, remained a rallying cry. The Apprentice Boys of Derry Association, originally eight Parent Clubs in the city, had since 1945 expanded its network of clubs across Northern Ireland; Terence O'Neill, Brian Faulkner and the Minister of Home Affairs, William Craig, were all members. For a brief period, from January 1920 until 1923, the city had a nationalist-controlled Corporation and Mayor under the system of Proportional Representation, but with its abolition unionists returned to power. In 1936, the government approved a restructuring of ward boundaries which gave unionists control of the Corporation and remained essentially in place until 1968. The Waterside ward on the east bank of the river Foyle with a Protestant majority returned four unionist councillors. The South ward, taking in the Catholic Bogside and Brandywell elected eight nationalists. Crucial to the electoral arithmetic was the North ward, which brought together the walled city, the strongly Protestant working-class Fountain, the mixed Rosemount district and middle-class Protestant streets to elect eight Unionists. Unionists were given a further advantage by the voting system in local government elections whereby the franchise was exercised only by occupiers and their spouses. Although this did disenfranchise poorer Protestants, its effect fell disproportionately on large Catholic families with children living at home. The effect of these measures can be seen in the following calculation for 1967:

	Nationalist voters	Unionist voters	Seats˙
North ward	2,530	3,946	8 unionists
Waterside ward	1,852	3,697	4 unionists
South ward	10,047	1,138	8 non-unionists
Total	14,047	8,781	

This situation lay at the heart of the sense of discontent in the city's Catholic population. Not only did it seem palpably unjust; it impacted directly on the vital area of public housing. The extent and quality of Northern Ireland's public housing stock had long lagged behind the rest of the United Kingdom. While the impact of this was borne by the less advantaged sections of both communities, it was particularly keenly felt in the working-class Catholic areas of Derry where inadequate and overcrowded housing nursed frustration and discontent. Londonderry Corporation had a building programme but it did not keep pace with the problem. Moreover, since houses meant local election votes nationalists saw the building of the Creggan estate and the Rossville Street flats, both in the South ward, as a device to maintain the unionist majority in the electorally crucial North ward.

By the mid-1960s, Derry's nationalists had also come to believe that O'Neill's government was following a deliberate policy of discriminating against the city, and against the west of Northern Ireland generally. Evidence seemed to come from the policies pro-duced by the government's own reports. The Benson report on the railways resulted in the closure of the city's westerly rail link to Portadown, and almost in the severance of the entire rail network. One result of the Matthew and Wilson reports was the building of a new town and growth centre, Craigavon, beside Protestant Porta-down. What finally ignited anger in the city was the recommendation in 1965 by the Lockwood Committee that Northern Ireland's second university should be located in the largely Protestant market town of Coleraine. Derry's Magee University College, which had admitted its first students exactly 100 years before, was to close. This blow to the city's battered self esteem and employment prospects resulted in a popular protest which in many respects was a foretaste of what was to come three years later. The University for Derry Committee organised a mass motorcade to Stormont led by Eddie McAteer and the city's unionist mayor. It was an alliance across the religious divide which was fated not to last. The best that could be achieved was a link between Magee College and The New University of Ulster at Coleraine, which admitted its first students in October 1968. The loss of the university was not the last blow the city was to suffer, however. In 1967 one of its major employers, Monarch Electric, closed.

While these problems were particularly acute in Derry, similar complaints were being echoed elsewhere; Catholics believed that the unspoken agenda was to force continuing high levels of Catholic emigration. Of the various strands which came to articulate these feelings, one of the first was in Dungannon which exhibited many of the problems of Londonderry Corporation. In May 1963, Patricia and Conn McCluskey, a social worker and her doctor husband, formed the Homeless Citizens' League to protest about public housing provision and allocation. The following January they were instrumental in bringing about the Campaign for Social Justice, a group of educated Catholics who believed they could do a better job of highlighting discrimination than the Nationalist Party. In Derry the university issue had galvanised people as nothing before. Chair of the committee and organiser of the motorcade to Belfast was a young teacher from St Columb's College, John Hume. The son of an unemployed shipyard worker, Hume represented the generation whose potential had been opened up by the 1947 Education Act which had enabled him to attend St Columb's College, and thence move to higher education at Maynooth. Contemporaries at St Columb's, Seamus Deane and Seamus Heaney, were to become two of the most original and seminal figures in contemporary Irish literature, the latter winning the Nobel Prize. As a young teacher, Hume's first involvement was in community affairs rather than in politics; he became active in the Credit Union which sought to ease the housing situation for working-class families through a system of self-help. Even so, early indications of his political cast of mind were two articles he published in the *Irish Times* in 1964 in which he castigated northern nationalist leaders for their lack of constructive leadership. On a very different tack, but focusing on the same issues, was the Derry Housing Action Committee, led by the fiery young socialist, Eamon McCann, whose members began to disrupt meetings of Londonderry Corporation from the public galleries.

The Northern Ireland Civil Rights Association (NICRA) was in no small measure a product of the rethinking going on within republicanism, much of which was taking a Marxist direction. Social action was seen as a necessary prelude to a successful political strategy. The year 1964 saw the formation of Wolfe Tone Societies, formed to honour the memory of the United Irish leader. Two years later, at a conference of these societies, the NICRA was formed. Over the next few months, the new body expanded to bring in trade unionists, members of the Communist Party and Catholics who were already engaged in civil rights issues.

What brought the NICRA on to the streets was a series of incidents in the village of Caledon near Dungannon, which, unsurprisingly, involved housing. A young Protestant woman, single though engaged, was allocated a house. This brought into focus the accumulated sense of discontent. To draw attention to the issue, the young Nationalist MP for the area, Austin Currie, squatted in the house until evicted by the police. The immediate result was the announcement of a civil rights march from Coalisland to the centre of Dungannon. Although the police initially raised no objection, opposition to the march entering the town square began to emerge in the unionist community. The march, estimated at some 2,500 and including Austin Currie and Gerry Fitt, was halted at a police barrier beyond which were potentially hostile counter-demonstrators. After listening to speeches, the marchers ended their protest. But it had set a precedent for civil rights activists to follow, notably in Derry where the atmosphere was much more combustible. The fact that the police had noted the names of republicans helping to steward the march may well have contributed to subsequent decisions.

The initiative to hold the next civil rights march in Derry on 5 October 1968 came from Eamon McCann and the Derry Housing Action Committee. The proposed route was from the Waterside railway station to the Diamond inside the walled city. Its destination defied the convention by which 'nationalist' parades did not take place within the city walls, while to start the parade in the largely Protestant Waterside could be interpreted either as a desire to emphasise the nonsectarian nature of the event or as a deliberate challenge to unionists. The Apprentice Boys of Derry announced that their association would be holding an annual initiation parade on the same day and over the same route. Since 1964, the Liverpool Murray Club had come to Derry for that particular weekend and, accompanied by a band, had paraded back to the station after the initiation ceremony in the Apprentice Boys Memorial Hall. On 3 October, the Minister of Home Affairs, William Craig, banned all parades in the Waterside and within the walled city. In the event, the ban served only to increase the publicity for the march and its potential for confrontation, with far-reaching consequences. The crowd of several hundred which assembled in the Waterside on the afternoon of 5 October included Gerry Fitt, Eamon McCann and, with some reservations, Eddie McAteer and John Hume. Three British Labour MPs and television cameras were there to observe and record the event. What they saw and broadcast changed the course of Northern Ireland's history. When the march attempted to get under way, the police used their batons to stop and then disperse it. Both Fitt and McAteer were injured. The filming of this, and the subsequent use of water cannon, brought Northern Ireland into the forefront of public affairs. It also ignited a more general nationalist anger. By the evening of 5 October, there was serious rioting in the Bogside.

The new pace of the events was soon apparent. On 9 October, a march of about 3,000 organised by Queen's University students attempted to reach City Hall in Belfast. In the aftermath of this a new student radical group, the People's Democracy, was formed which over the next few weeks conducted protests in Belfast. In Derry the initiative passed from the radicalism of McCann's Derry Housing Action Committee to a body called the Derry Citizens' Action Committee. Its organising committee included John Hume and others, like Paddy Doherty and Michael Canavan, who were to transform the city's politics. An early indication of this was the marginalisation of the Nationalist Party, only one of whose members was on the committee. Its moment of triumph came on 16 November when a march estimated at over 15,000 crossed Craigavon bridge and entered the walled city in defiance of a government ban. The RUC knew it had to acquiesce. O'Neill was now in a dilemma. In one way the civil rights protest eased his path to reform – he had long known that the position of Londonderry Corporation was untenable – but it was also stirring strong emotions in his own party with key figures including William Craig believing that the movement was a thin cover for republicanism. In the event, he was left no choice. On 4 November, O'Neill, Craig and Faulkner were brought to London and told of Harold Wilson's insistence on reforms. If nothing was done, financial sanctions would follow. The reforms were announced on 22 November: the abolition of Londonderry Corporation in favour of a development commission, a points system for housing allocation, amendments to the Special Powers Act, the appointment of a complaints commissioner, and a review of local election suffrage. Had these been announced earlier, they might have been seen as an act of some statesmanship, but coming as they did after the 16 November march they merely seemed a capitulation to events on the streets. The influential civil servant Kenneth Bloomfield later perceptively noted that unionism constantly tried to buy reform at the previous year's prices.

This is not how it was seen by O'Neill's unionist critics. On the streets the reaction was being led by the Reverend Ian Paisley. On 30 November, he organised a mass protest in the centre of Armagh against a civil rights march in the city. More ominous was the open dissent of William Craig, who questioned the reform programme in a series of public speeches. On 9 December, O'Neill appealed directly to the public in a television address. 'Ulster stands at the crossroads', he began, and then asked the viewers what kind of society they wanted. At the heart of his broadcast was the message that Northern Ireland would best be served by a united community respected by the rest of the United Kingdom. His bitterest criticism was reserved for those within unionism who seemed to be arguing for a weakening of the British link. The appeal appeared to have some effect. Civil Rights protests were suspended, tens of thousands responded to an appeal by the *Belfast Telegraph* to support O'Neill and on 11 December he felt confident enough to sack Craig.

While the civil rights movement as a whole was willing to allow O'Neill some breathing space, the radicals of the People's Democracy were not. On 1 January 1969, some 80 of its members began a march from Belfast to Derry with the aim of forcing more reforms. The leaders were aware that Protestants would react against an invasion of their rural heartland but seriously misjudged the scale of what would happen. As they approached Derry on 4 January, they were twice attacked by groups of loyalists armed with cudgels and clubs, at Burntollet and the Irish Street estate on the Waterside. Injuries were considerable, the marchers believing that the police had given them inadequate protection and that off-duty members of the USC had been among their attackers. When the remnants of the march entered the city centre, severe rioting broke out. That night there was a police incursion into the Bogside in which discipline appears to have broken down, with attacks on individuals and damage to property. The results of these events cannot be overestimated. Not only was the brief truce heralded by O'Neill's broadcast at an end; so was any residuum of trust between Derry nationalists and the RUC. Barricades were erected and the words 'You are now entering Free Derry' painted on a gable end in the Bogside's Lecky Road. Another portent was a new sectarianism entering the city, beginning a process which within a few years was to see far-reaching changes in its demographic structure.

Faced with these events, the bonds holding together the Ulster Unionist Party began to snap. On 15 January, O'Neill announced the appointment of an enquiry into the events of the past months. This provoked the resignation of Brian Faulkner and another cabinet minister. O'Neill saw no alternative but to appeal to the electorate. The campaign for the election on 24 February 1969, the last in Stormont's history, saw both established power blocs in turmoil. The most dramatic result was that in Foyle where John Hume defeated Eddie McAteer. Two other Nationalist MPs were defeated by civil rights activists, heralding the party's demise. O'Neill, hitherto unopposed in Bannside, was run close by Ian Paisley, standing as a Protestant Unionist. Unionist constituency parties were bitterly fractured. O'Neill gained the support of 24 Unionists and three Independent Unionists, while 12 Unionist MPs were hostile or uncommitted. While a few middle-class Catholics campaigned for 'O'Neillite Unionists', there was no evidence that significant numbers had been won over. The fracturing of unionism, so long feared by its leaders, had happened. Two events served to administer the *coup de grace* to the stricken prime minister. The first was the election to Westminster for the Mid Ulster constituency on 17 April of the 21-year-old student Bernadette Devlin, whose revolutionary presence had an electrifying presence on the British House of Commons, and, indeed, on the world's media. The second was a series of explosions at electricity stations and water pipelines which the police linked with the IRA. The explosions were, in fact, the work of loyalists determined to see an end of O'Neill and all his works. On 28 April, he resigned.

6

The Troubles begin

The fortunes of the Unionist Party, and of Northern Ireland politics generally, might just have been different if O'Neill had been succeeded by his ablest critic, Brian Faulkner, but by one vote Unionist MPs elected instead Major James Chichester-Clark. Chichester-Clark's task was unenviable. Belfast had not featured prominently in the tumultuous winter of 1968–1969 but since the two communities there had been deeply affected by events, this was now to change. Tensions in parts of west and north Belfast came to a head at the end of the annual Twelfth of July processions when serious rioting occurred. This was an ugly portent of what was soon to happen in the city, but in the event it was Derry which once more provided the flashpoint. The occasion was the annual parade of the Apprentice Boys to commemorate the raising of the siege in 1689. This had often been a tense affair but in 1969 it held all the potential for disaster, especially after the funeral on 19 July of Samuel Devenney, a Bogside man who had been assaulted by police in his home in April. His funeral proved the signal for the formation of a new body, the Derry Citizens Defence Association, the avowed aim of which was to defend nationalist areas from police and loyalist incursions but which also included republicans keen to hasten the destabilisation of Northern Ireland.

On the afternoon of 12 August, as the Apprentice Boys clubs made their way through Waterloo Place on the edge of the Bogside, stones were thrown, initiating disturbances which were to grow in intensity over the next two days. The 'Battle of the Bogside', as it came to be known, stretched the police to the limit of their capacity. On the afternoon of 14 August, men of the Prince of Wales Own Regiment deployed on the edges of the Bogside. Their presence calmed the situation but also set Northern Ireland's affairs on a new course. Serious though the situation in Derry had been, it was only a prelude to something that informed observers had feared for months, widespread sectarian rioting in Belfast. Two things provided the immediate trigger. The first was an appeal on 13 August by leaders in the Bogside for assistance in diverting police resources from Derry, a call heeded by some civil rights activists. The second was a broadcast by the Taoiseach, Jack Lynch, that his government could no longer stand by, creating hopes among nationalists and fears among unionists, both illusory, that the Irish army was about to intervene.

The rioting in west and north Belfast on the night of 14–15 August demonstrated the extent to which the fabric of Northern Ireland had unravelled. As rival crowds clashed in the narrow streets between the Shankill and the Falls, a Protestant, Herbert Roy, was killed by gunfire. The police responded with machine-gun fire from armoured cars, in the course of which a nine-year-old Catholic boy, Patrick Rooney, was killed in his home. Particularly intense sectarian rioting spread in the Ardoyne where three-fifths of the houses in Bombay Street were burned out by a Protestant mob. Order was only restored, with some difficulty, by the deployment of two army battalions. Although much of Belfast remained quiet, there were serious disturbances in Newry, Armagh, Dungannon and Dungiven. In the course of these events, 10 people had died, eight in Belfast, and one each in Armagh and Dungiven. Property damage, especially in the affected areas of Belfast, was extensive. Moreover, in a development which was to gather momentum in succeeding years, 1,505 Catholic families and 315 Protestant families in Belfast were, through fear or direct intimidation, forced to move.

The importance of these events cannot be overstated. What had happened was nothing less than the political fracturing of Northern Ireland. With troops deployed on the streets, Harold Wilson's government, however reluctantly, had become inescapably involved in Northern Ireland's affairs. The first clear sign of this was the Downing Street Declaration, issued on 19 August after meetings between the British premier and Chichester-Clark. It attempted to address a civil rights, rather than a nationalist, agenda. The border was not an issue; instead, there was to be equality of treatment and freedom from discrimination for everyone in Northern Ireland. The pace of reform was set by Home Secretary, James Callaghan, who received sanction for his actions by the publication in September of the Cameron Report into the disturbances of the previous winter. In preparing his findings, Lord Cameron had accepted many of the indictments made by the civil rights movement. The report was ill received by unionists who could see how it pointed to the erosion of cherished positions. Confirmation of their suspicions quickly followed with the recommendations of Lord Hunt's committee of enquiry into the police on 3 October. Central to Hunt's analysis was that any threat to Northern Ireland's security should be the responsibility of the Westminster government. He advised that the RUC should be relieved of all its military duties and be disarmed. The Ulster Special Constabulary was to be replaced by a locally recruited security force under army command, the Ulster Defence Regiment (UDR) as it was soon termed. The furious loyalist reaction to the Hunt report, especially to the abolition of the USC, led to serious rioting in Belfast, in the course of which, by a cruel paradox, a young policeman, Victor Arbuckle, became the first member of the security forces to be killed. The disbanding of the USC fatally undermined the credibility of Chichester-Clark's government with the unionist community and helped spur the formation of other loyalist groups.

Further dimensions of the British reform programme included the establishment of a Ministry of Community Relations and measures relating to fair employment. Any hopes for a peaceful political evolution foundered on the complex fall-out from the events of the previous August, not least the crystallisation of thinking within republicanism. During the riots the IRA had not been conspicuous in the defence of nationalist areas either in Derry or Belfast, while the British government's involvement was both a challenge and an opportunity for republicans. Although the sight of British soldiers on the streets ran counter to everything republicanism stood for, their presence indicated just how vulnerable the Stormont government had become. Further pressure might complete its collapse, opening the way to a united Ireland. Such feelings surfaced as early as 24 August when a group of disgruntled Belfast republicans met to devise a way of replacing the existing left-wing IRA leadership. Their chance came in December when a secret meeting of IRA leaders endorsed a political strategy which combined ending the established policy of abstentionism with the creation of a National Liberation Front linking Sinn Féin with left-wing groups. In response to this a Provisional IRA Council was set up. On 11 January 1970, the movement publicly split when the dissidents left the Sinn Féin Ard Fheis in Dublin to form their own provisional executive. The following month, the Provisionals, as they quickly became known, extended their organisation to Derry. Their immediate priority was the defence of nationalist areas, but a further intention was to take the offensive once conditions were favourable. Unlike the previous IRA campaign, recent events had politicised the nationalist community. If clashes were to recur, then the Provisional IRA was well placed to attract recruits. Not everything went the new organisation's way. The Official IRA also began to recruit, with areas of core strength in Derry and in the Lower Falls and Markets areas of Belfast.

On the other side of the political divide, the problems facing unionism multiplied. In April 1970, standing as Protestant Unionists, the Reverend Ian Paisley and the Reverend William Beattie won Stormont by-elections, Paisley winning O'Neill's old Bannside seat. Paisley's appeal to the unionist electorate was soon confirmed in the Westminster general election in June when he also took the strongly Protestant North Antrim seat from the sitting Unionist MP. His ability to attract support far beyond the ranks of his Free Presbyterian Church meant that the leaders of established unionism were compelled to take him into account when fashioning their political strategy; their power of manoeuvre was inhibited. April 1970 also saw the formation of the Alliance Party, which challenged unionism on a different flank. Alliance set out to recruit support from those who believed in non-sectarian politics. Although it wanted to make a fresh start, the party inevitably attracted many 'O'Neillite Unionists', including two Stormont MPs, as well as liberal Catholics. Although never making the electoral breakthrough its founders hoped for, it consistently attracted moderate voters from the two religious communities.

In August 1970, the final new element in the political structure came into place with the formation of the Social Democratic and Labour Party (SDLP). The formation of a new party was in many respects a natural sequel to the victories of John Hume and others over Nationalists in the February 1969 election. It was Hume who took the initiative in driving forward a new political alignment, though in terms of leadership he had to defer to the claims of Gerry Fitt. Not only was Fitt more experienced, his leadership was deemed essential if the new party were to avoid the Nationalist Party's fate of lacking a Belfast base. Hume provided much of the intellectual direction, especially on the issue of Irish unity and the nature of community division. Other prominent recruits included the Nationalist

MP Austin Currie, and the trade unionist Paddy Devlin. Combining such diverse elements, the SDLP declared itself to be a socialist party which aimed to achieve a united Ireland with the consent of a majority of people 'in the North and in the South'; in short it saw unity as conditional on the agreement of a majority inside Northern Ireland. Despite tensions in its leadership, and problems of sustaining a secure base in Belfast, the party quickly established itself as the undisputed voice of constitutional nationalism.

Changes were also taking place in high politics and on the ground. The British general election of June 1970 saw the Conservatives returned. It was soon clear, however, that under Edward Heath the old cosy relationship between Conservatism and Unionism had gone. Heath's government took office just as the 'marching season' was about to bring communal tensions once again into sharp focus. The first sign that this might happen came in April with rioting in the nationalist Ballymurphy area of west Belfast, when Protestants were driven from the small New Barnsley estate. In late June, three men and the two young daughters of one of them were killed in the premature explosion of a bomb they were making in Derry. Then, on 27 June, rioting broke out following an Orange parade in north Belfast. As rioting spread to east Belfast, the Provisional IRA began active operations from St Matthew's Church in the Newtownwards Road in defence of the nationalist Short Strand enclave. In heavy firing in both areas, five Protestants and one Catholic were killed.

The immediate response to this marked another decisive step in Northern Ireland's descent into civil strife. On 3 July the army imposed a curfew on the Lower Falls, with some 3,000 troops engaged in house searches. Both IRAs responded and five people were killed. The 'Lower Falls Curfew' effectively ended the period when the army could be seen as the defender of nationalist areas, though this had been steadily eroding for months. Instead, working-class nationalists increasingly responded to the Provisionals' message that only they could provide defence. Although rioting continued over the summer, the next six months saw the Provisional IRA build up its strength. Within the security forces there was an uneasy collaboration between a demoralised RUC and an army forced to adjust to a role for which it had neither training nor experience. On 6 February 1971, the army suffered its first casualty when Gunner Robert Curtis was shot dead in Belfast. The murder of two RUC officers in Belfast on 26 February led to the force being rearmed. The shooting of three young off-duty Scottish soldiers, two of them brothers, on 10 March removed any doubts that Northern Ireland had entered a new phase. The furious loyalist reaction to this led directly to Chichester-Clark's resignation 10 days later.

His successor, Brian Faulkner, represented unionism's last best hope. The able and ambitious son of a Co. Down clothing manufacturer, Faulkner had made his reputation as Minister of Commerce under O'Neill when he had helped induce a number of international companies to invest in Northern Ireland. His premiership marked a departure from the 'big house', landowner-dominated, unionism of Brookeborough, O'Neill and Chichester-Clark, so castigated by Ian Paisley. But more than many unionist politicians, Faulkner had cultivated his roots in the Orange Order. In the mid-1950s, he had helped lead Orangemen along the Long Stone Road, a Catholic town-land in Co. Down, not a record which nationalists remembered with affection. Faced with a deteriorating security situation, Faulkner set about the difficult path of combining reform with repression. On 22 June, he proposed a structure of three parliamentary committees, two of which would be chaired by opposition politicians. Initially welcomed by SDLP politicians, the proposal was smothered by events in the streets. In July, the Provisional IRA in Derry, which had somewhat lagged behind its Belfast counterpart, intensified its campaign against army posts. Faulkner had already widened the circumstances in which the security forces could open fire. On 8 July, two young Derrymen, Seamus Cusack and Desmond Beattie, were killed by the army. No evidence was produced to sustain the army's claim that they had been engaged in armed activity. The shooting, the first of its kind in the city, had important consequences. The first was an SDLP demand that unless there was an official enquiry, the party would withdraw from Stormont. When nothing was forth-coming, the party announced its withdrawal, despite reservations on the part of Fitt and Devlin. In doing so, Hume challenged the British government to take strong political action. The backdrop to this was an increase in Provisional recruiting in Derry and continual violence in the city.

Faced with this, Faulkner turned to what he believed was his only option, internment. His belief in its efficacy was based on his experi-ences of its use in the previous IRA campaign, but took insufficient account of the very different circumstances of the 1970s and the fact that this time the Dublin government would not be helping. Nor did the security forces have sufficient accurate intelligence about the Provisionals to make it effective. In the morning of 9 August, the army arrested 342 people. Many Provisional leaders had already taken evasive action, army lists were inaccurate or out of date, and one-third of those held were released almost immediately. The immediate result was a major upsurge in violence. Over the next three days 22 people were killed and thousands, mostly in north Belfast, fled their homes. Instead of dealing a mortal blow at the IRA, internment provided the spur to new recruitment. Nationalist anger was fuelled by allegations of ill-treatment of detainees during the internment operation. When Sir Edmund Compton reported into these in November, he found that interrogation techniques such as sleep deprivation, the playing of continuous noise between interrogations and the hooding and standing of suspects against a wall for between four and six hours constituted physical ill-treatment. The remaining months of 1971 saw a major bomb and gun offensive in Belfast, aimed at shattering the city's economy. During this period, 73 civilians, 30 soldiers, and 11 police and UDR were killed. Faulkner's government had played its last security option and lost, while the continuation of internment also closed off political advance since the SDLP refused political negotiations while it continued. By November, 980 had been arrested, of whom 504 had been released.

Unsurprisingly, this situation produced its own reaction in the loyalist community, which increasingly perceived the course of events since October 1968 as a sustained attack on Northern Ireland's constitutional position. There was also anger and resentment among working-class Protestants that housing and social conditions in areas such as the Shankill or Londonderry's Fountain were no better than those which had helped galvanise the civil rights movement. These feelings inevitably focussed on the perceived shortcomings of what had become a seriously divided Ulster Unionist Party. Since the most insistent critic was Ian Paisley, it was clear that many would look to him for a lead, but others were looking to figures within the Unionist Party, including William Craig. A broad-based coalition proved impossible; instead, in October 1971 Paisley announced the formation of the Democratic Unionist Party (DUP). He was joined by his colleague, William Beattie, and two Stormont Unionist MPs, John McQuade and Desmond Boal, an able and radical barrister. Under Paisley's charismatic leadership, the DUP rapidly made an established place for itself in unionist politics, though its strong personal links to the Free Presbyterian church did not always appeal to those in the other Protestant churches. In a quite separate development, a number of local vigilante groups which had formed in working-class Protestant areas came together as the Ulster Defence Association (UDA). The organisation adopted paramilitary uniforms and its parades, conducted in silence to military commands, were in icy contrast to the boisterous displays of traditional Orangeism.

Once again, however, the focus turned on Derry. In the aftermath of internment, barricades were again erected around the Bogside and the Creggan. 'Free Derry', as it was termed, was effectively under the control of the Provisional and Official IRA, the latter deeply involved in the working of the civil rights association. In January 1972, a new internment camp was opened at Magilligan near Derry. In response, the NICRA announced marches to be held at Magilligan on 22 January and in Derry on Sunday, 30 January. These were in defiance of a ban on all parades announced by Faulkner on 18 January. The Magilligan demonstration ended badly, with a violent confrontation between demonstrators and troops, including members of the Parachute Regiment. On Sunday, 30 January, a large crowd, possibly around 10,000, assembled in Derry's Creggan Estate, the intention being to march to Guildhall Square for a protest meeting against internment. Although the local RUC chief recommended against interfering with the march, it was decided to attempt to contain it within the Bogside. When a section of the crowd protested violently against this diversion, an arrest operation was launched by three companies of the Parachute Regiment. Shooting broke out in which 14 men were killed or mortally wounded. Although the army claimed that this was in response to firing, all the victims were unarmed. Nor were arms found. There were no army casualties. The abiding image of the day was that of Father Edward Daly, captured on television waving a bloodstained handkerchief as men carried one of the victims, Jackie Duddy. Few doubted that Northern Ireland had entered a new phase. In Dublin a large crowd burned down the British embassy. On 22 February, the Official IRA attempted to retaliate by bombing the officers' mess of the Parachute Regiment at Aldershot but only succeeded in killing five women workers, a gardener and a Catholic priest. In Derry anger over the event was compounded by the nature and conclusions of the official report of Lord Widgery which was published in April. Although Widgery conceded that in some cases 'firing bordered on the reckless', his report was regarded with contempt by nationalists as a whitewash of the army's actions. The immediate result in Derry was a further surge in IRA volunteers.

'Bloody Sunday' heralded the end of Stormont. Sensing that this was the case, William Craig sought to galvanise loyalist support through a new grass-roots movement, Ulster Vanguard. In a series of well-staged rallies in February and March 1972, Craig brought a number of senior Unionists and Orangemen together with the UDA and the Loyalist Association of Workers. His campaign was accompanied by attacks by both IRAs. As well as the Aldershot explosion, the Official IRA almost succeeded in assassinating the Minister of State at the Ministry of Home Affairs, John Taylor. Explosions in Belfast included those at the Abercorn restaurant, in which two women were killed and over 100 maimed and injured, and in Donegall Street, which killed six. No warnings were issued; indeed, in Donegall Street the casualties were increased by a misleading message. On 18 March, Craig addressed a mass rally of some 60,000 in Belfast. Amid rumours of Vanguard forming a provisional government, Craig spoke apocalyptically of the possibility of having to 'liquidate' their enemies. But if Vanguard hoped that in demonstrating their strength they could head off a major move by Heath's government, then they failed. London had reached the end of its tether.

From the previous August, when Heath's government had agreed to back internment, there had been signals that if the initiative failed, then, as Kenneth Bloomfield suspected, there would be fundamental questions. Well aware that the security situation had, in fact, seriously worsened and that Bloody Sunday had generated international pressure on London, Faulkner's government worked frantically on a package of reforms which might save the Stormont system. On 22 March, Faulkner, his deputy and leading civil servants flew to London to discuss these with Heath and his colleagues. For their part, the Conservatives were divided over whether to retain Stormont in some modified form. Faulkner was met by a demand that his government surrender all its security powers, that a Secretary of State for Northern Ireland be appointed, that moves to end internment be put in hand, and that negotiations begin for a community government. As Faulkner had already told Heath that, since the removal of law and order powers would fatally undermine his authority, his government would resign, the British move clearly signalled the end of Stormont. Faulkner's cabinet unanimously rejected the proposals. Two days later, Heath announced that the Northern Ireland parliament would be prorogued for one year. In fact, its meeting on 28 March proved to be its last. A two-day strike and a mass protest rally of some 100,000 at Stormont, addressed by Faulkner and Craig, showed the dimensions of the task the British government had set itself. If the political structure which had underpinned Northern Ireland for 50 years had been brought to an abrupt end, just what would replace it was ominously opaque.

7

Northern Ireland in crisis

While it was Northern Ireland which repeatedly caught the world's headlines, this should be set in the context of the Republic's economic and social transformation during the same period. In 1973, both parts of Ireland became part of the European Community. This led to the assumption that as the process of European union deepened there would be a lessening of division within the island. In fact, Irish governments became more enthusiastically 'European' than their British counterparts, and for good reasons. At one level, the Common Agricultural Policy was of considerable benefit to Ireland's farmers. In common with other economies, the industrial sector was badly affected by the world oil crisis of 1973–1974 but once economic recovery began, Ireland's position within the European Union left it well placed to attract inward investment. Imaginative investment in education in the 1970s was an added incentive. Two vocationally based universities, Limerick and Dublin City, brought fresh ideas into higher education, while the network of regional technical colleges, eventually thirteen in number, spread a trained workforce more widely across the country. By the 1990s, such firms in the vital new computer and electronics industry as Microsoft and IBM had made the Republic a major base of operations, a development which encouraged others to follow. Ireland was also one of the largest beneficiaries of the European Union's Structural Funds, designed to harmonise living standards across the Union. Between 1990 and 1997, the Republic received some IR£12 billion from the Structural

Funds, money carefully targetted upon economic development. By 1998, the Republic was becoming one of the fastest-growing regions of western Europe, with an economic self-assurance that stood in dramatic contrast to its northern neighbour. The economic and social transformation of the Republic forms an essential backdrop to the prolonged crisis north of the border.

Northern Ireland under Direct Rule

In British eyes the imposition of 'Direct Rule' from London in 1972 was never intended to be anything other than a temporary measure which would allow men and women of goodwill, the moderate centre which was assumed to exist, to reach political accommodation. This took inadequate account both of the bitterness and fragmentation in the unionist community as it contemplated the collapse of its cherished institutions and of the political inexperience of the Provisional IRA, which believed that the collapse of Stormont opened the way to the final push for a united Ireland. Political power rested with the Secretary of State, William Whitelaw, and his junior ministers, who had to learn both the intractable realities of Northern Ireland's polarised politics and the bitter divisions within each community. As ministers came and went over the years, increasing influence inevitably fell to the civil service now under the newly created Northern Ireland Office. For the moment, however, the initiative lay with Whitelaw who brought to this unprecedented office great energy, political experience, and force of personality.

One encouraging sign, though brought to a head by tragic circumstances, was the ending of the Official IRA's campaign in May. Their killing of William Best, a young soldier home on leave in Derry's Creggan estate, had provoked a furious reaction in the city. Not all Officials agreed with the decision; some joined the Provisionals while others in time formed the Irish National Liberation Army (INLA) which continued the campaign of violence. The reality was that the Provisional IRA was now effectively the voice of armed republicanism. For some time there had been unofficial contacts with the British government through a variety of intermediaries. The most effective of these was John Hume who believed the end of Stormont offered the chance for real political progress which was being squandered by the continuing violence. Whitelaw met the Provisionals' major pre-condition for a ceasefire, the granting of political status to their prisoners. On 26 June, the IRA began a ceasefire with the intention of entering into negotiations, emphasising their deadly effectiveness by killing three soldiers near Derry and a policeman near Newry as the hour of their cessation approached. On 7 July, senior Provisionals were flown to London for secret meetings with Whitelaw. Their demands, that the British recognise the right of the Irish people to self-determination, that British troops be withdrawn by 1975 and that IRA prisoners be amnestied, were dismissed. Each side was stating positions rather than negotiating. On 13 July, the IRA ceasefire ended.

When their campaign resumed, it did so with renewed intensity. In the afternoon of 21 July, over twenty bombs exploded in Belfast, where targets included a shopping centre and Oxford Street bus station. Nine people were killed and there were extensive injuries and damage. Three major bombs also went off in Derry. 'Bloody Friday' left Whitelaw no alternative but to authorise military action against the 'no-go' areas of Belfast and Derry. In a massive deployment of military force on 31 July, called 'Operation Motorman', the army entered both nationalist and loyalist areas of both cities. Predictions of widespread casualties were not realised, though two people were killed in Derry. But a stark tragedy took place in Claudy, a small town near Derry, where three car bombs exploded without warning, killing eight people. The effects of the day were a real setback to the IRA, which could no longer organise attacks as readily as before.

But the organisation was very far from defeated. In Derry, a concerted bombing campaign destroyed much of the city centre, with its Protestant-owned businesses and symbols, including in August 1973 the Walker Pillar overlooking the Bogside. To the Protestants of the city's west bank, it appeared nothing less than a campaign against them and they began steadily to leave. Although no official figures exist, between 1971 and 1991 some 7,000 left for the Waterside across the river Foyle or abandoned the city altogether. As Protestant churches closed, or were sustained only by congregations which crossed the river on Sundays, the city's character changed irrevocably. Only the small Fountain estate remained of the old North ward unionist community which had until recently controlled the city's fortunes. In Belfast, other large-scale population movements were taking place. It was a complex process. Intimidation played its part, as the IRA and the UDA battled for control of territory. So did fear, as people in isolated or mixed communities re-grouped to settle among the security of their co-religionists. By 1974, it is believed that between 30,000 and 60,000 people in greater Belfast had found it necessary to move house, one of the largest population movements in post-war Europe. The fear was real enough, as UDA members, using the cover-name Ulster Freedom Fighters (UFF), began to match the IRA, adding a new dimension to the conflict. The mortality figures for 1972, 323 civilians, 103 regular soldiers, and 41 RUC and UDR, tell their own grim story.

The shape of Whitelaw's thinking on the constitutional way ahead began to emerge in September at a conference in Darlington and in October with a Green Paper, *The Future of Northern Ireland*. Although the SDLP boycotted the conference, their thinking undoubtedly influenced the discussion paper which suggested that the minority should be given executive power, though this was not defined, and contained a section on 'The Irish Dimension' which said that any new arrangement for Northern Ireland had to take account of its relationship with the Republic. These ideas took firmer shape in March 1973. On 8 March, a referendum, intended to reassure unionists, was held on whether Northern Ireland was to remain within the United Kingdom; 591,820, or 57 per cent of the electorate, said it should. This was followed by a government White Paper on the future shape of devolved government. This proposed to set in place an assembly, which was later confirmed at 78 members, elected by pro-portional representation. From this would come an executive which would require support across both communities. Arrangements were also to be negotiated for cross-border cooperation. Although dis-appointed that the Irish Dimension was not more clearly spelled out, the SDLP broadly welcomed the proposals as the basis for a way for-ward. The response of unionism was another matter. The Democratic Unionists, the UDA and the Vanguard movement rejected the White Paper. Faulkner's instinct was to work within the White Paper's framework. He succeeded in having this accepted by the Ulster Unionist Council, but at the price of the secession of William Craig and his supporters to form the Vanguard Unionist Progressive Party. The disintegration of unionism seemed irresistible.

The implications of this emerged clearly when elections to the new assembly were held on 28 June. The moderate centre was shown to have limited appeal, with Alliance winning eight seats and the Northern Ireland Labour Party one. With 19 seats, the SDLP con-firmed its position as the effective voice of the nationalist community. The unionist electorate's verdict was fragmented but not ultimately difficult to read. Faulkner managed to get 24 supporters elected, but quickly lost two of these when one was killed in an accident and another was elected speaker. At least two of his team were essentially opposed to the White Paper and although one other unionist joined him, Faulkner could only really rely on a total of 21 votes. By contrast, unionists opposed to the White Paper, a loose but determined alliance of DUP, Vanguard and 'Unofficial' Unionists, numbered 26. The unionist electorate had declared against the White Paper proposals, albeit by a narrow margin. While Faulkner Unionists, the SDLP and Alliance commanded a majority of the electorate, it is difficult to avoid the conclusion that the precarious basis of Faulkner's position was not adequately taken into account in the coming months.

This, then, was the shape of Northern Ireland politics as political leaders struggled to find an acceptable structure. The first sign that they might do so came on 21 November 1973 when Whitelaw confirmed agreement on the shape of an executive. This was to have six Unionist, four SDLP and one Alliance ministers, with Faulkner as Chief Executive and Fitt as his Deputy. But danger signals were there. On the one hand, the SDLP was lobbying hard for an effective Council of Ireland to give firm shape to the Irish Dimension, and for the replacement of the RUC by a new police service. On the other, votes in the Unionist Party showed a dangerous erosion of Faulkner's position, with hostile Unionists finding a leader in Harry West, a former minister under both O'Neill and Faulkner. At this critical point, Whitelaw, who had massaged the political situation, was replaced as Secretary of State by Francis Pym. It was a curious decision, made for British political reasons, since negotiations on the final shape of a settlement were due to commence at Sunningdale in Berkshire on 6 December. Presided over by Heath, those taking part included the Unionists, the SDLP, and Alliance. The Fine Gael–Labour government was represented by the Taoiseach, Liam Cosgrave, and key ministers, including his Foreign Minister, Garret FitzGerald, and Conor Cruise O'Brien. The unionist opposition was not invited; neither, of course, was the IRA. The main flaw in the conference was the perilously narrow political base from which Faulkner was operating. Most of the pressure was on the Unionist delegation, with the British and Irish governments and the SDLP apparently assuming that Faulkner, steeped as he was in unionist politics, would not agree to something he could not sell in his own community. The conference agreed on a Council of Ireland, consisting of a Council of Ministers of 14 members, drawn equally from the Irish government and the executive. The Council was to have 'executive action' in eight areas: natural resources and the environment;

agriculture, forestry and fisheries; cooperative ventures in trade and industry; electricity; tourism; roads and transport; advisory services in public health; sport, culture and the arts. The only significant concession won by the Unionists was that the Council 'would act by unanimity'. Overall, the Sunningdale Agreement represented a considerable victory for the SDLP, or so it seemed.

Faulkner's weakness was soon cruelly exposed. On 4 January 1974, the Ulster Unionist Council rejected the Sunningdale proposals. Faulkner and his assembly supporters left the party to form their own organisation. Then, under intense pressure from the miners' strike in Britain, Heath called a general election. With neither head-quarters nor organisation, Faulkner's position was hopeless. In contrast, Harry West's Unionists, Craig's VUPP and Paisley's DUP formed the United Ulster Unionist Council, winning 11 of the 12 seats with an emphatic majority of unionist votes. It was a blow from which neither Faulkner nor Sunningdale ever really recovered. Although the executive struggled on under the new Labour Secretary of State, Merlyn Rees, opposition to the Council of Ireland was stirring in other quarters. On 14 May, as the assembly was due to pass a motion endorsing the new structures, a hitherto unknown body, the Ulster Workers Council (UWC) announced that a general strike would begin the following morning. Inspired in part by the miners' strike in Britain, which had effectively toppled Heath, in the spring of 1974 a group of workers in key factories and industries, notably Harland and Wolff, Shorts, and, crucially as it turned out, the electricity services and petroleum industry began to prepare for an industrial stoppage. Their leaders, none of whom were prominent public figures, formed a rather uneasy alliance with West, Craig and Paisley, and also with the loyalist paramilitary organisations, of which the UDA under Andy Tyrie was the largest. Chairman of the organising committee was a young Vanguard trade unionist from Londonderry, Glen Barr. Without much real organisation, these men were planning to defy not just the executive but the power of the British state; they took as their sanction the results of the February election.

The initial response to the strike call by an unprepared public was poor. The muscle behind the strike was provided by the paramilitaries, whose members systematically 'discouraged' people from remaining at work. By the end of the first day, major industries had closed and ferry services to Scotland had stopped. From then on, the stoppage developed its own dynamic. Adding to the sense of crisis, loyalist paramilitaries exploded a series of car bombs in the Republic, killing five in Monaghan and 22 in Dublin. Within days, Northern Ireland came to a halt as the UWC calibrated the electricity supply and the distribution of petrol. Members of the Protestant middle class, at first tepid or hostile towards the strike, increasingly rallied behind it, especially after a maladroit broadcast by Harold Wilson on 25 May when he castigated the strikers as those who spent their lives 'sponging on Westminster'. With the army apparently lacking the numbers to control the situation or the expertise to man the power stations, the British government and the hapless executive became bystanders. On 27 May, as the complete shutdown of the electricity network approached, Faulkner resigned. Parades and bonfires in Protestant districts celebrated the overthrow of the 'Sunningdale experiment'.

It is impossible to overstate the significance of what had happened. That effective power could be seized so completely by a group of unelected and largely unknown men was a measure of the widespread feeling among unionists that in adopting a Council of Ireland the Sunningdale Agreement had pushed them a step too far. Their success also marked the limitations of British power. From then on, it was generally agreed that a political solution had to come from within Northern Ireland. This left a major problem in finding agreement from a totally fragmented unionist community, not least because the UWC leadership had no political strategy beyond the overthrow of Sunningdale and quickly faded from view. Merlyn Rees sought to move matters on with the publication of a new White Paper on 4 July which proposed the election of a Constitutional Convention to find agreement on the political structure. While this was being done, a new IRA truce was observed from 22 December 1974 to 17 January 1975 and then an indefinite ceasefire from 10 February which officially ended on 22 September 1975. Once again, the IRA failed to induce the British government into setting conditions for a withdrawal, even though the organisation later claimed they had grounds for believing this was a possibility, something denied by British sources. Elections to the convention were not held until 1 May 1975. If the government hoped for any breakthrough by the 'moderate centre', then again their hopes were confounded. The Alliance Party won eight seats and the SDLP fell to 17, but the major failure was Faulkner's newly formed Unionist Party of Northern Ireland, which could only take five seats. It was the end for Faulkner and his brand of unionism. The winner in the convention election, with 47 seats, was the United Ulster Unionist Coalition, But the coalition was only really united in its opposition to Sunningdale, and stresses soon emerged. The most unexpected development was William Craig's advocacy of a form of power sharing with the SDLP, a conversion which led to his denunciation by Paisley and expulsion from the UUUC. In November 1975, the convention endorsed the UUUC position of a slightly modified return to a Stormont-type structure with no institutionalised links with the Republic. This was unacceptable to the government which wound up the convention in the spring. There was now no obvious political option, beyond the efficient and impartial operation of direct rule.

Even the Official Unionist Party, as it had become, continued to have its stresses. The October 1974 British general election had two significant consequences. The first was Harry West's defeat by an independent nationalist. The second was the election of the former Conservative cabinet minister Enoch Powell as Official Unionist MP for South Down. Possessed of a visionary sense of British nationality, Powell became a powerful voice within the party for full integration within the United Kingdom. This found an echo with the party's new parliamentary leader at Westminster, James Molyneaux. Unlike Harry West, Molyneaux had never sat at Stormont. Molyneaux's battlefield was the House of Commons, where Powell was an acknowledged master. Since Westminster was where Northern Ireland's affairs were being determined, Molyneaux's star rose as West's waned, while relations with the DUP, never straightforward, deteriorated. The UUUC's end came when the Official Unionists would not back a Paisley-led attempt to repeat a loyalist strike in May 1977.

With the collapse of the truce, the IRA campaign resumed, acquiring new dimensions. In March 1973, the Provisionals had begun a campaign in England with car bombs in London. This reached a climax on 21 November 1974, when 21 people were killed by bombs in Birmingham. Despite the operational difficulties, and the tensions bearing on the large Irish community working in Britain, the IRA were willing to sustain its operations in Britain because of the direct pressure they believed it put on the British government. Within Northern Ireland, in 1977 a series of attacks on businessmen seemed designed to undermine the economic structure, increasing the pressure on London to withdraw. Although there is no evidence that any businesses left, such tactics could not help attract new industries at a time when the vital synthetic fibre industry was being undermined by world economic forces. Internally, the IRA reorganised on a tight cellular structure, which recognised a lack of recruits but also made it virtually invulnerable to penetration by the security services. While its campaign against the army and police continued at a sustained level, other actions seemed overtly directed against the civilian population, notably the murder of 10 Protestant workmen at Kingsmills in south Armagh in January 1976, and the killing of 10 people in an incendiary attack at the La Mon House Hotel in Co. Down in February 1978. On 27 August 1979, the IRA campaign reached a peak with the assassination of Lord Mountbatten, a member of the royal family and last Viceroy of India, in Co. Sligo, together with three members of his party, and the blowing up of 18 soldiers near Warrenpoint in Co. Down. On a different level, a realisation that a British withdrawal was not, after all, imminent was leading some republicans to articulate a more wide-ranging and imaginative political agenda. Central to this development were the writings of Gerry Adams, then an internee, who published a series of anonymous letters in *Republican News* between 1975 and 1977.

The loyalist paramilitaries were also intensifying their campaign. The Kingsmills massacre of Protestants was apparently a belated response to the murder of three members of the Miami Showband by the UVF in July 1975. Between 1972 and 1979, a group which became known as the 'Shankill Butchers' struck fear in parts of west and north Belfast for the ferocity of its attacks, which included Protestants as well as Catholics. Popular revulsion at the continuing level of violence found a focus in the marches and rallies of the Peace People, which attracted tens of thousands in Belfast, Derry and Dublin in the summer of 1976. But although the efforts of the organisers, Mairead Corrigan and Betty Williams, earned them the Nobel Prize for Peace, the momentum could not be sustained. It was an honourable, but ultimately rather sad, attempt to voice a yearning for a more normal society. So, too, was the appeal of the new Pope, John Paul II, at Drogheda in September 1979 to those engaged in violence to 'return to the ways of peace'.

The British general election of May 1979 brought mixed signals. The new Prime Minister, Margaret Thatcher, was something of an unknown quantity, though she was known to have been strongly influenced by the ideas of Enoch Powell and by her pro-unionist Northern Ireland spokesman, Airey Neave, who had been killed by the INLA weeks before the Conservative election victory. She herself confessed to profoundly unionist instincts. In Northern Ireland, the results made the Official Unionists look increasingly vulnerable, with the DUP's Peter Robinson and John McQuade taking East and North Belfast, and James Kilfedder in North Down leaving the party. The following month, the first elections to the European parliament saw a triumph for Ian Paisley, who recorded a massive 170,688 votes. John Hume came a respectable second with 140,622, but the Official Unionists performed dismally. John Taylor took the third seat with 68,185, but Harry West failed with 56,984 and resigned as leader. It was the nadir of their fortunes. The task of rebuilding the Ulster Unionist Party as the established voice of unionism fell to James Molyneaux. A cautious and courteous man, strongly based in the Orange and Black Institutions, Molyneaux worked hard to raise his party's fortunes at the grass roots, and believed that he could use his influence with the new, and apparently more sympathetic, government at Westminster. The size of Hume's vote also seems to have focussed tensions which had been simmering in the SDLP leadership, though the actual occasion of the change of leadership was the publication of a new set of British proposals which seemingly ruled out discussion of an Irish dimension. Fitt, who wished to negotiate on that basis, resigned as leader, to be replaced by Hume, for whom the Irish dimension was fundamental to any settlement. The vision of Northern Ireland's future held by the two new party leaders, Molyneaux and Hume, could not have been more starkly different, but in any event the political features of Northern Ireland were soon to be changed in the most dramatic manner by the unfolding events in the Maze prison.

The hunger strikes and their consequences

In 1976, the government announced that it was ending the special category status for paramilitary prisoners which Whitelaw had introduced. This was part of a wider policy of 'Ulsterisation' under which security primacy passed from the army to the RUC. The attempt to impose prison conditions met with a determined rejection by republican prisoners who refused to accept that they were criminals. By 1978, they were engaging in the 'dirty protest', which involved smearing their cells with excrement and menstrual blood. The initiative lay with the prisoners. A hunger strike which began in October 1980 was called off after fifty-three days when it seemed that concessions might be forthcoming. When they were not, on 1 March 1981, the IRA commander in the Maze prison, Bobby Sands, began a hunger strike. Sands was followed at intervals by others, including the INLA Maze commander, Patsy O'Hara. The tense situation acquired an unexpected dimension with the death of the Independent MP for Fermanagh-South Tyrone. In the resulting by-election, Sands defeated the Unionists' Harry West. On 5 May, Sands died, his funeral being attended by an estimated one hundred thousand people. In what had become a grim war of attrition between the republican prisoners and the government, a further nine hunger strikers died. On 3 October, after intense mediation by senior Catholic churchmen working with hunger strikers' families, the hunger strike was called off. Special category status was not reintroduced, but the main demands of the hunger strikers were quietly implemented. Although Thatcher later claimed that the events had been a defeat for the IRA, the facts indicate otherwise. That ten men had consciously starved themselves to death, showed the depth of their commitment. Sands's election victory opened up new prospects. In August, this was confirmed when Provisional Sinn Féin's Owen Carron, standing as a Proxy Political Prisoner, retained the seat. The hunger strikes had changed the face of Northern Ireland politics in a way its originators could scarcely have imagined, but at the human cost, not just of the hunger strikers, but of a milkman and his son stoned by protestors in Belfast, two young girls killed by plastic bullets, and a woman census collector shot dead in Derry.

The first public indication that the two election victories might spur republicanism in new directions came at the Sinn Féin Ard Fheis on 31 October when Danny Morrison voiced a possible strategy based upon the ballot box and the armalite rifle, opening the way for the party to fight elections. The test would be whether Sinn Féin could build sufficiently on its core support to challenge the SDLP's dominance of nationalist politics. Vindication of the new direction seemed to come in October 1982 in elections for a new assembly when Sinn Féin won 64,191 first preference votes compared with 118,891 for the SDLP. Although both the London and Dublin governments were alarmed at the strength of the Sinn Féin vote, in fact it carried a mixed message. While Sinn Féin's appeal was undoubtedly to a section of the electorate which had never been attracted to the SDLP, it could not be denied that the latter had polled substantially worse than Hume's 1979 European election total. The British general election of June 1983 brought Sinn Féin a further boost when Gerry Adams won West Belfast, defeating the SDLP's Joe Hendron, with the sitting MP, Gerry Fitt, in third place. Adams's electoral victory, with its high international profile, was soon followed by his election to the Sinn Féin presidency.

One result of Sinn Féin's political success was a dawning community of interest between London and Dublin. Even here the process was not straightforward, since Margaret Thatcher was bitterly resentful over what she saw as the unhelpful attitude of Charles Haughey's Fianna Fáil government during the Falklands conflict in 1982. It fell to Haughey's Fine Gael successor, Garret FitzGerald, to find a way forward. FitzGerald had an ambitious agenda which had at its core a new British–Irish structure which would strengthen constitutional nationalism. Part of this would be a North–South court and police structure, but he also felt it necessary to air the concept of joint London–Dublin authority over Northern Ireland. These ideas were explored in the New Ireland Forum in which Fine Gael, Fianna Fáil, Labour and the SDLP thrashed out various options. When the Forum reported in May 1984, it set out three possibilities: a unitary Irish state, a confederation between north and south, and joint British–Irish authority. Rejection by unionists was, of course, inevitable but before the British government could give its definitive response the IRA intervened, to devastating effect. Since the death of the hunger strikers, Thatcher had been a priority target. In the early hours of 12 October 1984, as the prime minister was preparing her speech for the Conservative Party conference, a bomb exploded in Brighton's Grand Hotel, killing five people. The following month, after an Anglo-Irish summit, she sharply rejected the three Forum models, causing no small offence in Dublin. Anglo-Irish relations had touched their nadir, or so it seemed.

8

From the Anglo-Irish Agreement to the Good Friday Agreement

The British government was, nevertheless, prepared to negotiate on the basis of joint consultation with Dublin, in the hope of achieving greater security cooperation along the border. The Dublin government's aim of establishing some kind of joint policing was dismissed as impracticable, while joint courts foundered on the opposition of the judiciary. After months of intricate negotiation, to which the SDLP but not the unionists were privy, the Anglo-Irish Agreement was signed by Thatcher and FitzGerald at Hillsborough on 15 November 1985. The Agreement, an international treaty, enshrined the right of the Dublin government to be consulted on Northern Ireland issues through the creation of an Intergovernmental Conference headed by the Secretary of State for Northern Ireland and the Irish Foreign Minister. This was to be serviced by a permanent secretariat of civil servants from both jurisdictions working from Maryfield outside Belfast. Behind the Agreement lay the expectation that nationalists would see Dublin's formal involvement in Northern Ireland's affairs as at last giving them a voice in its affairs. What neither premier had adequately anticipated was the extent and fury of the unionist reaction, compounded as it was by their all too obvious exclusion from what was being negotiated. While some had believed the unionists would be shocked into negotiating for something better, more experienced hands such as Kenneth Bloomfield correctly predicted that it would simply drive unionism into a resentful laager.

On 23 November, unionism's feelings were exposed when Molyneaux and Paisley addressed a protest rally estimated at 200,000 in
Belfast city centre. The subsequent campaign against the Agreement,
strident and at times violent, could do nothing to remove it. Unionist
MPs resigned their seats to force a referendum on the Agreement but
the vote at the consequent by-elections was smaller than they had
hoped, while they lost Newry and Armagh to the SDLP's Seamus
Mallon. Frustrations reached their peak at Portadown over the issue
of the right of the loyal orders to parade through the nationalist
Tunnel area of the town. There was serious violence between loyalists
and the RUC at Easter and in July 1986, with the Orange Order's
church parade being re-routed from the Tunnel to the apparently
less contentious Garvaghy Road. It was a dangerous portent of what
was to happen 10 years later. These events stimulated recruiting into
the UVF and UDA, and with the IRA dismissing the Agreement as
reinforcing partition, Northern Ireland's chances of political stability
seemed as distant as ever. For many nationalists, however, the Agreement seemed to signal that the British government was prepared to
intervene on their behalf and the 1987 general election showed a
strengthening of the SDLP, not least in dismissing Enoch Powell in
South Down. Even so, Sinn Féin's core support remained intact at
11 per cent of the electorate, with Adams retaining his seat with an
increased majority.

The three years after the Agreement were characterised by a series of
events which showed the capacity of all sides to sustain the conflict,
seemingly indefinitely. In April 1987, Lord Justice Maurice Gibson
and his wife were killed by a bomb as they were crossing the
border. The following month, the British army's Special Air Service
(SAS) killed eight members of the IRA's elite East Tyrone brigade
as they attacked Loughgall RUC station. On 8 November, an IRA
bomb killed 11 people at a Remembrance Day service at Enniskillen.
It was a propaganda disaster for the organisation, not least because of
the dignified response of Gordon Wilson, father of one of the victims,
who declared his forgiveness of the bombers. The intensity of the
conflict was confirmed by a grisly sequence of events which unfolded
in Gibraltar on 6 March 1988 when three unarmed IRA members,
Mairead Farrell, Sean Savage and Daniel McCann, were shot dead
by the SAS. At their funerals in Belfast, a loyalist gunman, Michael
Stone, killed three people, including IRA member Kevin Brady. At
Brady's funeral, two British army corporals, Robert Howes and
Derek Wood, were surrounded and killed when their car approached

the cortège. Confirmation of the IRA's ability to sustain a 'long war' came in November 1987 when the *Eksund* was intercepted off the French coast with a large consignment of sophisticated weaponry from Libya. Any elation felt by the security forces was quickly sobered by the revelation that this was the last of four such shipments.

Such events understandably masked developments on the political front which were to acquire a growing, if often unsteady, momentum. Aware that the Anglo–Irish Agreement had been directed against them, the Sinn Féin leadership moved to develop and refine their political strategy. In November 1986, Adams secured a major revision of Sinn Féin policy when the party's Ard Fheis voted to end the policy of abstentionism from the Dáil. Opponents of the decision, led by Ruairí Ó Brádaigh and Daithi Ó Connaill, seceded to form Republican Sinn Féin. The Sinn Féin leadership had now effectively passed to northerners such as Adams, Tom Hartley and Martin McGuinness who could see the need for new political directions which would build on wider nationalist alliances across Ireland. Such an initiative was not long in coming, since in January 1988 John Hume began a process of dialogue with Adams and the Sinn Féin leadership which lasted until the autumn. In this the SDLP confronted Sinn Féin with their belief that Britain no longer retained any military or economic interest in remaining in Ireland. They also asked whether Sinn Féin accepted a number of key propositions: that the Irish people had the right to self-determination; that the Irish people were deeply divided on how to exercise that self-determination; and that the agreement of both unionist and nationalist traditions was essential. In response, Sinn Féin argued that, in effect, there was insufficient evidence of Britain's neutrality towards Irish unity and that the unionist minority in Ireland could not be allowed to veto the right of the Irish people as a whole to self-determination. The exchanges, though inconclusive, explored substantive issues and laid the basis of a positive relationship between Adams and Hume.

This was a period when violence continued at a high level, if more selectively than in the 1970s. The IRA's capacity to strike extended to Britain and continental Europe, with attacks on British servicemen in the course of which two Australian tourists were killed. In July 1990, Thatcher's friend and unionist supporter, the Conservative MP Ian Gow, was murdered. The following January, the IRA came close to killing the British cabinet with a well-executed mortar bomb attack on Number 10 Downing Street. A bombing campaign clearly designed to shake Britain's financial will to continue the fight reached a peak in 1991–1993. In April 1992, bombs at the Baltic Exchange in the heart of London's financial centre killed three people and caused damage estimated at £800 million. Almost exactly a year later, a similar attack at the NatWest Tower caused one death and even greater damage. From December 1991, car bombs caused devastation in the centres of Belfast, Craigavon, Derry, Newtownards, Banbridge, Portadown, Bangor, Coleraine and Magherafelt. Attacks were also directed at civilians associated with, or carrying out work for, the security forces; in January 1992, seven Protestant building workers were killed at Teebane in Co. Tyrone.

The campaign was matched in intensity by the UVF and UFF, whose strategy was to make the republican movement, and the nationalist community in general, question the price in human terms of the IRA campaign. The surge in loyalist violence also reflected a deep sense of alienation felt in Protestant working-class communities in the wake of the Anglo-Irish Agreement. In February 1992, the UFF claimed, as its response to the Teebane massacre, an attack on a bookmakers' shop on Belfast's Ormeau Road which killed five Catholics. In March 1993, four Catholic building workers, one of whom belonged to the IRA, were killed in Castlerock Co. Londonderry. A sustained series of attacks was also directed at Sinn Féin workers. It was a grim period of mutual retaliation in which north Belfast and mid-Ulster acquired a particularly fearful reputation. In October 1993, Northern Ireland touched its nadir. On 23 October, nine innocent people were killed when a bomb exploded in a Shankill Road fish shop in what was apparently a botched IRA attack on the UFF leadership. One of the bombers also died. Both the UFF and the UVF responded, the former with an attack on a bar in Greysteel near Derry, killing six Catholics and one Protestant. With 27 people killed that month, such was the depth of fear in both communities that political and religious leaders were conscious that Northern Ireland had the prospect of violence on the scale of the former Yugoslavia.

Throughout this period, attempts were being made at various levels to work towards a resolution of the conflict. On the British side, the prime mover was Peter Brooke who became Secretary of State for Northern Ireland in 1989 and was responsible for sending out a number of important signals to Sinn Féin. In November 1989, Brooke stated in an interview that the security forces could not defeat the IRA and that the government would respond imaginatively in the event of a ceasefire. He also drew an analogy with Cyprus where the British had withdrawn two years after using the word 'never'. A year later, in November 1990, he publicly reinforced Hume's message to Sinn Féin that Britain had 'no selfish or strategic or economic interest in Northern Ireland'. Three weeks later, Thatcher was replaced by John Major who was to bring considerable personal commitment to the Northern Ireland problem. Finally, on 26 March 1991 Brooke defined in parliament the nature of government thinking on the broad framework of an agreement. Negotiations would take place on the basis of three key, and mutually interlocking relationships, or 'strands'. Strand One would be concerned with a devolved administration in Northern Ireland, Strand Two would focus on North–South structures, while Strand Three would discuss the relationship between the United Kingdom and the Republic. Talks in 1991–1992 involving the British and Irish governments, the Ulster Unionists, the SDLP, the DUP and Alliance produced no agreement, but the three Brooke strands remained tenaciously embedded in all subsequent British initiatives.

Progress now developed on a number of fronts, focussing on how Sinn Féin could be brought into the political process based on a cessation of the IRA campaign. Given the intensity of the violence, the IRA's innate suspicion of British intentions, and the predictable unionist reactions to such a development, the difficulties should not be underestimated. In 1990, the British government opened secret channels of communication to the Sinn Féin leadership. Then, on 16 December 1992, Sir Patrick Mayhew, who had succeeded Brooke as Secretary of State, in a major speech at the University of Ulster in Coleraine, conceded that there were leading Sinn Féin figures who wished to follow a constitutional path. 'Provided it is advocated constitutionally', he argued, 'there can be no proper excuse for excluding any political objective from discussion. Certainly not the objective of an Ireland united through broad agreement fairly and freely achieved.' In the following months, the British renewed their secret contacts with Sinn Féin, and, equally significantly, Hume and Adams continued their dialogue, encouraged by Albert Reynolds, the new Fianna Fáil Taoiseach. Central to their discussions was the principle that the Irish people had the right to self–determination, that there could be no internal settlement within Northern Ireland, and that while the consent of unionists would have to be obtained, the unionists could not have a veto over what happened. The climax of these events was the unveiling by Major and Reynolds of their Joint Declaration on Northern Ireland on 15 December 1993.

Unlike 1985, the British consulted Molyneaux and his colleagues in advance of the document. For its part, the British government confirmed that it had no selfish strategic and economic interest in Northern Ireland, and both governments gave an assurance that democratic political parties committed to 'exclusively peaceful methods' would be able to take part 'fully in democratic politics'. At the heart of the document was the idea of self-determination and how this was to be expressed. The British government agreed that it was for the people of 'the island of Ireland alone, by agreement between the two parts respectively, to exercise their right of self-determination on the basis of consent, freely and concurrently given, North and South, to bring about a united Ireland, if that is their wish.' This was a formula which was intended to reassure unionists while opening the door to republicans. While republicans would have wished for a statement that Britain had no 'political' interest in Northern Ireland, for many unionists the Declaration confirmed fears that London had no interest in the union at all. Unionists also objected that the concept of self-determination 'for the people of the island of Ireland alone' wrote off their sense of Britishness, central to their sense of identity.

The ceasefires and the peace process

As well as the secret contacts with the British government and the Hume–Adams dialogue, other influences were at work to encourage an IRA ceasefire. Not only was the Dublin government of Albert Reynolds engaged but so, too, were powerful voices in Washington. In 1992, in the course of his campaign for the Democratic nomination, Bill Clinton had indicated his willingness to appoint a special envoy to Northern Ireland. Some key advisers had a strong personal commitment to the pursuit of peace in Northern Ireland. In the wake of the Joint Declaration, advisers in the National Security Council, and influential Irish-American politicians, argued that the granting of a visa to Adams would help consolidate the Sinn Féin President's position by signalling Washington's independence from its British ally. Adams's subsequent visit to the United States, with its widespread media exposure, added considerably to his credibility. By the summer of 1994, the republican leadership was arguing that while its goal of a united democratic socialist republic remained unchanged, the republican movement did not have the strength to achieve this on its own. What it recommended was the pursuit of a nationalist consensus embracing the Dublin government and the SDLP, with the aid of

Irish-America, which would create the dynamic for fundamental change. On 31 August 1994, the IRA announced its 'complete cessation of military operations'.

These moves were paralleled by developments within the loyalist paramilitaries, who had long been disenchanted with the mainstream unionist parties. For a time the UDA flirted with the idea of negotiated independence, but it moved away from this and in 1987 published *Common Sense*, which argued for a power-sharing government with responsibilites allocated in proportion to the votes gained. In 1993–1994, while the UFF and the UVF continued a relentless campaign, the Combined Loyalist Military Command, representing both organisations, had set out its political thinking. This argued that there could be no diminution of Northern Ireland's place within the United Kingdom, but also defended the right of anyone to seek constitutional change by democratic and peaceful means, and accepted the possibility of North–South structures provided these did not amount to an interference with internal jurisdiction. These ideas were articulated by two political parties, the Progressive Unionist Party (PUP), close to UVF thinking, and the Ulster Democratic Party (UDP), which grew out of earlier UDA political initiatives. The PUP leaders, Gusty Spence, Billy Hutchinson and David Ervine, and the UDP's Gary McMichael and Ray Smallwoods represented a new voice within loyalist politics, which survived Smallwoods's assassination by the IRA in July 1994. Peace moves were brokered by influential Protestant clergymen. Reassured that there had been no secret deal between the British and Sinn Féin on Northern Ireland's constitutional status, on 13 October 1994 the Combined Loyalist Military Command announced the end of its 'operational hostilities'. With republican and loyalist ceasefires in place, the way seemed clear for substantive political progress, though no one doubted the chasms of distrust which would have to be bridged. The pace of events was further affected by a governmental crisis in the Republic which saw Albert Reynolds, who had been deeply involved in events, replaced by a new Fine Gael–Labour coalition led by John Bruton.

It was not until 22 February 1995 that Major and Bruton revealed their 'Frameworks for the Future', which were intended to set an agenda for political discussions. The first Framework, which set out a possible governmental structure, envisaged an assembly of around 90 members elected by proportional representation. Contentious legislation would require a weighted majority, and a separately elected three-member Panel would have 'important consultative, monitoring, referral and representational functions'. The second Framework suggested North–South institutions which would have 'executive, harmonising and consultative functions'. Executive functions might extend to: sectors involving a natural or physical all-Ireland framework; European Union programmes and initiatives; marketing and promotion activities abroad; and culture and heritage. Harmonising functions included: aspects of agriculture and fisheries; industrial development; consumer affairs; transport; energy; trade; health; social welfare; education; and economic policy. The consultative role of the North–South body would be to exchange information about 'existing and future policy' with a view to 'common or agreed positions'. The primary objective behind these proposals was 'to promote and establish agreement among the people of the island of Ireland, building on the Joint Declaration'. Despite assurances from Major and Mayhew that the Framework proposals left the union intact, the prevailing view in unionism was that they were being asked to move too far in terms of all-Ireland bodies. While it was true that the language of the Frameworks paid little respect to unionist sentiment, paragraph 16 made it clear that 'the democratic right of self-determination by the people of Ireland as a whole must be achieved and exercised with and subject to the agreement and consent of a majority of the people of Northern Ireland'. Since the combined voting strengths of the SDLP and Sinn Féin fell short of that majority, it was possible for the veteran analyst Keith Kyle to argue that it was 'a pro-partitionist document heavily disguised in language that falls more easily to the lips of Republicans'.

While it was now clear what shape the two governments wanted a settlement to take, two issues began to assume an increasing importance, each disturbing the course of events. The first was that of the decommissioning of paramilitary arms. To the British government, and the unionists, the decommissioning of IRA weapons became a condition of all-party talks including Sinn Féin. For their part, Sinn Féin leaders made clear their view that this would be tantamount to a surrender, that Sinn Féin and the IRA were separate organisations, and that the British government had not made decommissioning the precondition to talks. Decommissioning was to become the most intractable issue of all. The second problem was associated with parading, something with tenacious roots in Ulster society, especially so on the Protestant side. By 1995, it was a growing phenomenon. That year there were 3,500 parades, compared with 2,120 in 1985. Of the 1995 total, 2,581 were identified with 'loyalism', in the form of the Orange Order, the Royal Black Institution, the Apprentice Boys of Derry or local band parades. Most were uncontroversial, trouble occurring at only 13, but it was trouble out of all proportion. Confrontation focussed on certain areas where 'traditional' loyalist parading routes passed through, or near, areas where the population had become nationalist as a result of population movement. Chief among them was Portadown where the return route of Portadown District Loyal Orange Lodge from their annual service at Drumcree Parish Church took in the nationalist Garvaghy Road, whose residents formed the Garvaghy Road Residents Coalition. Each side claimed rights. While the Orangemen claimed the right to march, the residents argued for the principle of consent. What to nationalists were displays of Protestant triumphalism, to Orangemen were cultural or religious expressions. Nationalists argued that 'parity of esteem' was an essential ingredient in the new political climate. Orangemen countered that it was their culture which was under challenge. There was no meeting of minds. On 9 July 1995, nationalist protestors assembled on the Garvaghy Road. Two days later, as the Orangemen refused to leave Drumcree and widespread protests in support of them took place, a local agreement permitted the parade down the road. Both Ian Paisley and the local Ulster Unionist MP, David Trimble, were closely involved, meeting the Orangemen on their return to the town centre.

Trimble's high profile, and identification with what was termed the 'Siege of Drumcree', turned to his advantage the following month when James Molyneaux, whose political base had been undermined by the Framework Documents, announced his resignation as leader of the Ulster Unionist Party. On 8 September 1995, the Ulster Unionist Council elected Trimble as leader. Then aged 51, Trimble represented the coming of age of a new generation within unionism; moreover, as a former law academic at Queen's University he had an analytical mind and a sharp eye for detail, qualities which would be tested in the negotiations which lay ahead. By that time, the IRA ceasefire had been in place for a year, though political progress still seemed a distant prospect. On 28 November, Major and Bruton agreed a strategy for all-party talks combined with the establishment of an international body to be chaired by the former American Senator George Mitchell to report on arms decommissioning. Two days later, President Clinton arrived in Northern Ireland in a major presidential gesture designed to cement the peace process. When Mitchell's group reported on 24 January 1996, it suggested a compromise by which some arms decommissioning would be carried out at the same time as political negotiations. The report also suggested that all parties in the negotiations should commit themselves to 'democratic and exclusively peaceful means of resolving political issues', to the 'total disarmament of all paramilitary organisations', and to 'agree to abide by the terms of any agreement reached in all-party negotiations'. Major's response to the Mitchell proposals was to announce that elections would be held to a new political Forum which would provide each party with a democratic mandate. While the decision was welcomed by unionists, the SDLP and Sinn Féin denounced it as both unnecessary and setting a new precondition to all-party talks. On 9 February 1996, the IRA ended its ceasefire with a car bomb at London's Canary Wharf which killed two and caused widespread damage. The bomb reflected the IRA's view that after 17 months of ceasefire, political progress still seemed remote.

When the elections to the Forum were held on 30 May, the UUP came out ahead of the DUP, with 30 seats to 24. With 17 seats to the SDLP's 21, and its highest vote at 15.5 per cent, Sinn Féin seemed more than ever a serious challenger. Because of the list system employed, the PUP and UDP gained seats, as did the Women's Coalition and Robert McCartney's United Kingdom Unionist Party, thus entitling them to take part in negotiations. Since Sinn Féin was excluded because of the lack of an IRA ceasefire, and the SDLP stopped attending in September, the Forum never developed any real identity, though political talks chaired by Senator Mitchell did begin. What the Forum debates did confirm was the continuing chasm within unionism over the direction of political progress.

At this time of apparent political stalemate, community tensions escalated alarmingly as the result of a recurrence of the previous year's trouble over Drumcree. On 7 July 1996, as the police attempted to re-route Portadown District's return parade away from the Garvaghy Road, confrontation recurred which lasted until 11 July. During this time violence on a serious scale broke out, including the murder of a Catholic taxi driver in neighbouring Lurgan. Faced with a fast-deteriorating situation in loyalist districts throughout Northern Ireland, on 11 July the RUC reversed their decision, allowing the parade to proceed down the Garvaghy Road, albeit under various conditions. This, in turn, led to widespread rioting in nationalist areas. Far from engaging in a peace process, the summer of 1996 saw relations between the two communities as bad as they had ever been. Disputes over parades erupted in other places, while certain nationalist areas saw boycotts of Protestant-owned businesses. In this sour atmosphere, when the talks resumed in September they were clearly in the doldrums. The winter of 1996–1997 saw scant progress. The main development was the working of the committee under Dr Peter North, which the government established to review the issue of parading. Its central recommendation, when it reported on 30 January 1997, was for a Parades Commission to make legally binding recommendations over disputed parades, though this was not implemented in time for the 1997 'parading season'. The vexed issue of parades continued to expose the raw emotions, and deeply held convictions, which lay behind political division. Although John Major was strongly committed to political progress, his government was fast running out of political authority as parliamentary by-elections steadily eroded his majority and his party squabbled over Europe. On 1 May 1997, the British political picture changed dramatically with the overwhelming victory of Tony Blair's Labour Party. Unlike Major, Blair had an unassailable parliamentary base from which to operate.

His Secretary of State, Dr Marjorie Mowlam, soon had to confront the bitter realities of Northern Ireland street politics, for which 'Drumcree' had become the shorthand. On 6 July 1997, the government went for the 'least worst option', forcing the Portadown Orange church parade along the Garvaghy Road under heavy security force presence. Loyalist relief was palpable. Nationalist opinion was outraged. Such was the intensity of feeling on both sides over what was likely to happen during the main Orange Order parades on 12 July that informed observers felt that civil war was a possibility. Once again, Northern Ireland showed itself able to pull back from the edge of an abyss, though only just. On 10 July, to an almost universal sense of relief, the Orange Order announced that its four most contentious parades would not take place. The remaining Orange parades on 12 July proceeded virtually without incident. That Northern Ireland had passed a point of crisis became clearer 10 days later when the IRA announced the renewal of its ceasefire.

The Good Friday Agreement

When negotiations resumed in the autumn under Senator Mitchell, they took a new form. Sinn Féin, the PUP, the UDP and the Women's Coalition took part, as did the UUP, the SDLP and Alliance, while the DUP and the United Kingdom Unionists did not.

Since between them the DUP and United Kingdom Unionists represented 40 per cent of the Protestant electorate, much would turn on the stance taken by David Trimble's Ulster Unionists, and on Trimble's subsequent ability to sell any agreement to his supporters. The attitude of the PUP and the UDP would also be crucial, given their influence in working-class loyalist communities. With the gulf of distrust between unionism and republicanism, negotiations were difficult. The Agreement finally brokered by Mitchell was concluded on 10 April 1998, Good Friday, only after substantial personal involvement by Blair and his Irish counterpart, Bertie Ahern, with encouragement from President Clinton.

While its essence retained the now familiar three strands, there were moves in the unionist direction from the terms of the Framework Documents. The Agreement acknowledged that while a substantial section of the people of Northern Ireland shared the legitimate wish of the people of the island of Ireland for a united Ireland, the present wish of the people of Northern Ireland, freely exercised and legitimate, was to maintain the Union and: 'accordingly, that Northern Ireland's status as part of the United Kingdom reflects and relies upon that wish; and that it would be wrong to make any change in the status of Northern Ireland save with the consent of a majority of its people'. The basis of the Union was set firmly on consent; this was seen both as a guarantee to unionists and a confirmation to nationalists that Britain had no other interest in Northern Ireland. The formula enabled Sinn Féin to see the Agreement as a transitionary phase to Irish unity. To facilitate both political traditions, certain constitutional changes were to be made. On the British side, the 1920 Government of Ireland Act, which had embodied British jurisdiction and partitioned Ireland, was to be repealed. For its part, the Republic agreed to repeal Articles 2 and 3 of the 1937 Constitution.

The Agreement set out new principles for the internal government of Northern Ireland through a 108-member Assembly, elected by proportional representation. Governmental responsibilities would be allocated according to party strength in the Assembly and mechanisms were set in place to ensure that key decisions would have cross-party support. Such decisions would require either a 'majority of those members present and voting, including a majority of the unionist and nationalist designations present and voting; or a weighted majority (60 per cent) of members present and voting, including at least 40 per cent of each of the nationalist and unionist designations present and voting'. The Assembly was to have both legislative and executive powers, though Westminster retained the power to legislate for Northern Ireland. The Executive was to be headed by a First Minister and a Deputy First Minister, elected on a cross-community basis. They would preside over an Executive Committee allocated to parties on the basis of the number of seats they held in the Assembly. Those elected to office had to be pledged to democratic, non-violent means.

Such complex mechanisms were a reassurance to nationalists that there would be no return to the unionist-dominated system which had operated down to 1972. Nationalists also had their Irish identity and aspirations acknowledged through the creation of a North/ South Ministerial Council, drawn from the Assembly and the government in Dublin. Decisions were to be by agreement, an essential condition for unionist support. It was to deal with matters of potential all-Ireland interest, such as aspects of agriculture, transport, tourism, and educational qualifications. Finally, there was to be a British/Irish Council, representing the British and Irish governments and the Northern Ireland Assembly, as well as the devolved parliaments in Scotland and Wales. This would deal with such issues as transport links, cultural issues and the environment.

Further elements dealt with human rights and equality, the latter critical to Sinn Féin's support. In particular, the British government pledged itself to 'take resolute action to promote the (Irish) language'. Other aspects were less palatable to unionists. The Agreement set out arrangements for an independent Commission 'to make recommendations for future policing arrangements'; this clearly involved the future of the RUC. The section on the decommissioning of arms required all parties 'to reaffirm their commitment to the total disarmament of all paramilitary organisations', and 'to use any influence they have, to achieve the decommissioning of all paramilitary arms within two years'. Equally problematic for many unionists was the section on prisoner releases, vital if Sinn Féin, the PUP and the UDP were to endorse the proposals. This set out a schedule for advancing the release dates for prisoners belonging to paramilitary organisations and observing a ceasefire, and certainly within two years. Finally, all the various elements in the Agreement were 'interlocking and interdependent'; parties would not have the luxury of choosing which parts they accepted.

It was a complex Agreement in which arguably nationalism had made the greater compromises. If pro-Agreement unionists and loyalists argued that the Union had been secured, pro-Agreement nationalists and republicans could portray the equality agenda as ensuring that in time demographics would deliver a united Ireland. But the SDLP and the great majority of Sinn Féin supported it, as did the Alliance Party and the Women's Coalition. The endorsement of the PUP and UDP delivered the support of a crucial section of working-class loyalism. The DUP and United Kingdom Unionists were resolutely opposed, seeing the Agreement as a fatal undermining of the Union. While Trimble secured the backing of his party's ruling council, there was a potentially dangerous erosion of support within mainstream unionism. Just before the conclusion of the negotiations, some members of his negotiating team, including Jeffery Donaldson MP, had been reluctant to follow him into acceptance. Other Ulster Unionist MPs in the House of Commons, led by William Thompson, MP for West Tyrone, baulked at supporting the Agreement. With a majority of unionist MPs in the Parliament ranged against the Agreement, there were serious doubts about its acceptance by the Protestant electorate. As the referendum approached, it was clear that SDLP and Sinn Féin supporters would overwhelmingly endorse the Agreement, while Ian Paisley, Robert McCartney and William Thompson of the UUP led an intensive campaign against it. As polls privately indicated a large measure of unionist unease, Trimble supporters at times feared the outcome. In the end, it took the substantial personal commitment of Blair on the issues of decommissioning and prisoner releases to reassure wavering unionists. When the referendum was held in Northern Ireland on 2 May, the Agreement was endorsed by 71.2 per cent of the electorate. Support in the Republic was even more emphatic. Irish nationalism and republicanism had backed the Agreement. The figures seemed to show that unionists had also done so, albeit by a narrow margin and with reservations. The level of support among unionists, deeply unhappy over prisoner releases and wary over decommissioning, remained problematic, though supporters of the Agreement could point to the overall desire in the electorate to give the deal a fair wind.

The Assembly elections, held on 25 June, broadly confirmed this picture. Of the pro-Agreement parties, the UUP won 28 seats, the SDLP 24, Sinn Féin 18, Alliance six, the PUP two, and the Women's Coalition two. For the opponents, the DUP won 20, the United Kingdom Unionists five, and independent Unionists three. The UDP, which backed the Agreement, failed to secure representation, and the PUP did less well than it had hoped. Even so, there was a substantial pro-Agreement majority in the Assembly. The First Minister designate, David Trimble, was in the potentially difficult position of commanding a unionist group of 30, UUP and PUP members, against a combined unionist opposition grouping of 28. This reflected continuing unease in the Protestant electorate over the Agreement. Trimble's Deputy, the SDLP's Seamus Mallon, had a rather more secure mandate.

Despite the Agreement, tensions within the community remained high, not least over the issue of parading. In July the newly established Parades Commission ruled against the Portadown Orangemen returning from Drumcree church along the Garvaghy Road. The following days and nights saw escalating tension between loyalist supporters and the police in Portadown and elsewhere. The climax came with the death of three young Catholic boys in Ballymoney. But the confrontation in Portadown remained stubbornly unresolved and festered throughout the subsequent winter months. Even less predictable was the reaction of sections of the IRA which were opposed to a settlement giving less than a united Ireland. It was such dissident republicans, calling themselves the Real IRA, who exploded a major bomb in Omagh's town centre on 15 August, killing 29 people and two unborn children. Such was the scale of the reaction across Ireland, and elsewhere, to this atrocity that even this group suspended its operations. Omagh became the symbol of what all sections of Northern Ireland's population had endured over almost three decades. No one pretended that Northern Ireland remained other than a deeply polarised community, overwhelmingly united in a desire for peace but still uncertain as to how it might be achieved.

9
Reflections and conclusion

Because of its prolonged nature and special interest to much of the English-speaking world, the conflict in Ireland has produced a vast literature, both academic and polemical. Nowhere is this better studied than in John Whyte's magisterial survey, *Interpreting Northern Ireland*, published in 1990. Although there have been important contributions to the literature since that date, there is no need to revise Whyte's basic framework which identifies 'Traditional Nationalist', 'Traditional Unionist', 'Marxist', and 'Internal Conflict' interpretations. While the last two offer important insights, the Nationalist and Unionist interpretations are at the heart of the problem. The Nationalist interpretation rests fundamentally on the view that Ireland is a single nation, defined by geography, and entitled to self-determination. Britain is seen as the historical impediment to the achievement of that ideal. Central to the Unionist interpretation is that Ireland is home to two nations, each entitled to self-determination. While the Nationalist focus is on the island of Ireland, Unionists look to the archipelago, to them the British Isles. The emphasis on self-determination is not new. It featured strongly in British discussions of Ireland's political future in 1919–1920, when the American President Woodrow Wilson's doctrine of self-determination dominated the Paris Peace Conference. Its continuing centrality can be seen in the Hume–Adams dialogue, as well as the various British and Irish policy documents of the 1990s. At the heart of the Good Friday Agreement lies the statement that it was for the people of the island of Ireland alone, 'by agreement between the two parts respectively and without external impediment, to exercise their right of self-determination on the basis of consent, freely and concurrently given, North and South, to bring about a united Ireland, if that is their wish, accepting that this right must be achieved and exercised subject to the agreement and consent of a majority of the people of Northern Ireland'.

Whatever view we take of these contrasting positions, few would contest that minority questions have been central to the course of events. Just as northern unionists feared becoming a minority of some 25 per cent in an all-Ireland state, northern nationalists felt frustrated and marginalised within Northern Ireland. Part of the growing self-confidence of the Catholic community in Northern Ireland was the comfort of rising numbers; 34 per cent of the population in 1922, by the 1990s the Catholic proportion was around 43 per cent. Differentials remained between the two communities. A Catholic unemployment rate in 1998 of 16 per cent compared with that for Protestants of 9 per cent, but strict Fair Employment legislation, introduced in 1976 and strengthened in 1989, precluded any return to systematic discrimination. This was reflected in the growth of the Catholic professional and commercial middle class; between 1990 and 1998 the proportion of Catholics in the professions had risen from 33.4 per cent to 40.6 per cent. Such figures need to be treated with care, since unemployment rates in both Protestant and Catholic working-class areas remain stubbornly high, with all the associated social and health problems. The minority question was compounded by that of mixed populations, the issue which nationalists had been led to believe the Boundary Commission would address. J. J. Lee argued that while unionists had a case for certain areas being excluded from a Dublin parliament, they had no case for some of the areas they acquired. Patrick Buckland believed that any border would have been unsatisfactory to some nationalist or unionist wishes and that the basic flaw in Northern Ireland lay in the type of devolved government established in Belfast.

Economic circumstances have changed beyond recognition since 1922. From being an agricultural appendage of Britain, by the 1990s the Republic was seen as one of the most dynamic areas of the European Union. Its commitment to Europe was confirmed when, unlike the United Kingdom, it joined the European Monetary Union in 1999. Northern Ireland's economic fortunes had gone the other way. Once a vibrant outcrop of the British economy, it had become a highly subsidised dependent. When British Secretaries of State

84

declared that Britain had no economic interest in remaining in Northern Ireland, they were telling the truth. This was an uncomfortable reality behind the political negotiations.

The Northern Ireland conflict always presented a complex picture. The total number of deaths, 3,289, together with an injury total of 42,088, must be set against a small population of some 1,675,000 in 1997. Even so, some have argued that one reason why the conflict lasted so long was that Northern Ireland never descended to the level of inter-community conflict of Lebanon or Bosnia. Certain areas, north and west Belfast, south Armagh, mid-Ulster and the Fermanagh border region, saw a disproportionate level of violence, with families living in real fear for much of the time. Derry, which featured prominently in the early phases of the conflict, saw a decline in violence long before Belfast did. But large parts of Northern Ireland witnessed violence only intermittently, if at all. In such areas, a comfortable middle-class lifestyle could be maintained. While professional salaries were on a par with the rest of the United Kingdom, living costs were lower. A much-repeated criticism was that the middle class largely opted out of politics. This undoubtedly reflected the fact that Northern Ireland politics were more dangerous than elsewhere, but it was also a feature of the so-called democratic deficit. The fact that political outlets were largely confined to the 18 Westminster seats, and largely powerless local authorities, meant that a political career held out few inducements. In contrast, the paramilitary groups on both sides found their recruits overwhelmingly from young working-class males, something which bred its own resentments.

The Good Friday Agreement, supported by the two sovereign governments and over 71 per cent of the Northern Ireland electorate, represented a major step in political evolution, something acknowledged by supporters and opponents alike. It was attempting nothing less than a fundamental redefinition of the political shape of Ireland as it had emerged in 1922. But it was not an end in itself. Nor was everyone reconciled to what had been concluded. The Omagh bomb was a demonstration of how some republican dissidents felt. Unease was more widespread in sections of the unionist population, many of whom voted for the Agreement with reservations. The unionist electorate was almost equally divided on the merits of the political settlement. If the old structure of Northern Ireland had broken down on the disaffection of its nationalist minority, the new one potentially had the problem of a large minority of dissident unionists. No one doubted that the future held challenges as well as opportunities. The people of Northern Ireland overwhelmingly desired peace and a sense of normality but they remained deeply divided, rallying to different symbols of national allegiance and indentity. Marching as they did to very different tunes, a true sense of reconciliation had still to be worked for.

Further reading

General reading

J. Bardon, *A History of Ulster* (The Blackstaff Press, Belfast, 1992). An extended account of the political, social and economic dimensions.

P. Bew and G. Gillespie, *Northern Ireland. A Chronology of the Troubles 1968–1993* (Gill and Macmillan, Dublin, 1993).

P. Bew and G. Gillespie, *The Northern Ireland Peace Process 1993–1996. A Chronology* (Serif, London, 1996). The two books by Bew and Gillespie are essential points of reference, with short interpretative essays which make them much more than chronologies.

S. J. Connolly, editor, *The Oxford Companion to Irish History* (Oxford University Press, Oxford, 1998). Another key work of reference and interpretation on events and personalities down to 1972.

R. F. Foster, *Modern Ireland 1600–1972* (Allen Lane, London, 1988). A major interpretation of Irish history which challenged many established assumptions.

T. W. Hennessey, *A History of Northern Ireland 1920–1996* (Gill and Macmillan, Dublin, 1997). Thorough account of political developments in the period.

J. J. Lee, *Ireland 1912–1985. Politics and Society* (Cambridge University Press, Cambridge, 1989). An extended analysis of the period, brimming with insights.

J. Loughlin, *The Ulster Question since 1945* (Macmillan, Basingstoke, 1998). An excellent guide to the issues.

C. Townshend, *Ireland The Twentieth Century* (Arnold, London, 1999). Clear introduction to the nature of Ireland's development.

J. H. Whyte, *Interpreting Northern Ireland* (Oxford University Press, Oxford, 1990). A classic work of scholarship.

More specialised studies

P. Arthur, *The People's Democracy 1968–1973* (The Blackstaff Press, Belfast, 1974). Well-informed contemporary account.

A. Aughey, *Under Siege. Ulster Unionism and the Anglo-Irish Agreement* (The Blackstaff Press, Belfast, 1989). Informed discussion of unionism at a time of crisis.

K. Bloomfield, *Stormont in Crisis. A Memoir* (The Blackstaff Press, Belfast, 1994). Memoirs of an influential civil servant, inevitably somewhat reticent but with acute insights.

P. Buckland. *The Factory of Grievances. Devolved Government in Northern Ireland 1921–39* (Gill and Macmillan, Dublin, 1979). Detailed account of working of Northern Ireland government.

B. Chubb, *The Government and Politics of Ireland* (Longman, Harlow, 3rd edition, 1992). Essential guide to the topic.

F. Cochrane, *Unionist Politics and the Politics of Unionism since the Anglo-Irish Agreement* (Cork University Press, Cork, 1997). Critical appraisal of unionism.

S. Dunn, editor, *Facets of the Conflict in Northern Ireland* (Macmillan, Basingstoke, 1995). Particularly useful essays on the cultural and social background.

R. English and G. Walker, editors, *Unionism in Modern Ireland* (Gill and Macmillan, Dublin, 1996). Illustrates different facets of unionism.

J. Hume, *Personal Views. Politics, Peace and Reconciliation in Ireland* (Town House, Dublin, 1996). Reflections of a key political figure.

N. Jarman and D. Bryan, *Parade and Protest. A Study of Parading Disputes in Northern Ireland* (Centre for the Study of Conflict, University of Ulster, Coleraine, 1996). Well researched and influential study.

K. A. Kennedy, editor, *From Famine to Feast. Economic and Social Change in Ireland 1847–1997* (Institute of Public Administration, Dublin, 1998). Useful set of essays, especially for nature of economic change.

K. Kyle, *A Framework for the North* (Centre for the Study of Conflict, University of Ulster, Coleraine, 1995). Analysis of key constitutional proposals; argues that unionists should be reassured by the proposals.

B. Lynn, *Holding the Ground: The Nationalist Party in Northern Ireland, 1945–72* (Ashgate, Aldershot, 1997). Thorough account of nationalist politics in the period.

E. Mallie and D. McKittrick, *The Fight for Peace. The Secret Story Behind the Irish Peace Process* (Heinemann, London, 1996). Well informed, with useful documents.

N. Ó Dochartaigh, *From Civil Rights to Armalites. Derry and the Birth of the Irish Troubles* (Cork University Press, Cork, 1997). Well researched study of the city's pivotal role.

H. Patterson, *The Politics of Illusion. A Political History of the IRA* (Serif, London, 1997). Penetrating analysis of the political evolution of republicanism in its various forms.

B. Purdie, *Politics in the Streets: the Origins of the Civil Rights Movement in Northern Ireland* (The Blackstaff Press, Belfast, 1990). Analyses the key developments of the 1960s.

J. H. Whyte, *Church and State in Modern Ireland 1923–1979* (Gill and Macmillan, Dublin, 1980 edition). Sophisticated analysis of a sensitive topic.

The familiar lines of the Morris Minor 1000, which made its debut at the Earl's Court Motor Show in October 1956.

THE MORRIS MINOR

Ray Newell

Shire Publications Ltd

CONTENTS

Published in 1998 by Shire Publications Ltd, Cromwell House, Church Street, Princes Risborough, Buckinghamshire HP27 9AA, UK. Copyright © 1992 by Ray Newell. First published 1992; reprinted 1993 and 1998. Shire Album 277. ISBN 0 7478 0149 5.

Printed in Great Britain by CIT Printing Services, Press Buildings, Merlins Bridge, Haverfordwest, Pembrokeshire SA61 1XF.

British Library Cataloguing in Publication Data: Newell, Ray. The Morris Minor. — (Shire Albums Series; No. 277). I. Title. II. Series. 629.222. ISBN 0-7478-0149-5.

Editorial Consultant: Michael E. Ware, Curator of the National Motor Museum, Beaulieu.

ACKNOWLEDGEMENTS
The author wishes to acknowledge the assistance of Roy Turner, Neville Wright and Roger Tennyson in locating specific photographs, and Jane White in the preparation of the manuscript. Photographs are acknowledged as follows: the BBC and John Podpadec, from the BBC-2 series *Perpetual Motion*, page 7; the British Motor Industry Heritage Trust, pages 4 (bottom), 5-6 (all), 10 (bottom), 11 (top), 12 (top) and 15 (bottom); and the National Motor Museum, Beaulieu, pages 1, 2, 14 (bottom), 16 (both), 17 (bottom), 18-21 (all), 25 (top) and 31 (both). The cover photograph is by Jon Colley Photography. The remaining photographs are from the author's collection.

Cover: *This immaculate 1966 Morris Minor 1000 Convertible owned by Mike Ameson was photographed in the village of Badger, Shropshire, by Jon Colley.*

Lord Nuffield (William Richard Morris) in his office at Cowley.

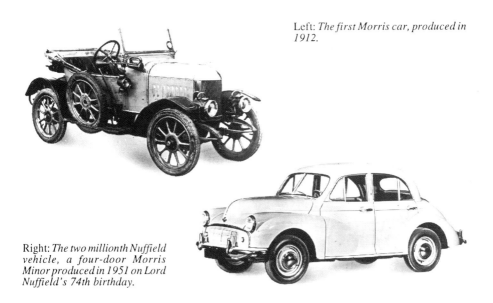

THE EARLY YEARS

The tradition of Morris vehicles dates back to the beginning of the twentieth century, when a young entrepreneur, William Richard Morris, developed his interest in motorcycles into a thriving sales and repair business in High Street, Oxford. Within a decade purpose-built premises, named the Morris Garage, had been established in Longwall Street, Oxford, and by 1913 Morris's long-held ambition to design and build his own car had been achieved. The car, the Bullnose Oxford, was the forerunner to many other famous models, including the Morris Cowley in 1915, the Morris Minor in 1928, the Morris Isis in 1930, the Morris Ten in 1933 and the Morris Eight in 1934.

The success of the Morris range was based on a hard-earned reputation for 'quality' motor cars and it brought financial security and public recognition for William Morris, who became a baronet in 1929, Baron Nuffield in 1934 and Viscount Nuffield in 1938. In the best traditions of business enterprise, Morris's company grew from its tentative beginnings in the cycle-repair trade, with a working capital of £4, into a multi-million-pound motor manufacturer. Lord Nuffield became well known as a public benefactor, making generous donations estimated at £30 million to medical and educational causes. His reputation as a shrewd, if sometimes uncompromising, businessman was aptly demonstrated in 1921 when, in the midst of a sales slump following spiralling post-war price increases and faced with rising costs, he cut the price of all Morris models by £100. As a result sales rose, the company drew ahead of its rivals and many new enterprises were bought or started. Morris Motors Limited expanded, Morris Commercial was established, the MG Car Company was formed and the original concern of Morris Garages Limited continued as a distribution centre. The Wolseley Company was acquired in 1927 and the Riley Company taken over in 1938. The manufacturing plants at Cowley and Abingdon near Oxford were expanded and many supporting component factories were established, including radiators and bodies branches and the purchase of the SU Carburettor Company. It was inevitable that they would eventually come under one umbrella organisation; this happened in 1940 with the formation of the Nuffield Organisation.

Left: *Sir Alec Issigonis, the much acclaimed designer of the post-war Morris Minor.*

Right: *Issigonis was a compulsive doodler. These early sketches bear a close resemblance to the final form of the production car.*

FROM CONCEPT TO REALITY: THE SERIES MM

It was at this time, at the beginning of the Second World War, that attention focused on the need to produce a new small Morris car. Under the guidance of Miles Thomas, Vice-chairman and Managing Director of the Nuffield Organisation, and Vic Oak, Chief Engineer at Morris Motors Limited, early plans were laid and the expertise of Alec Issigonis, a young engineer who had joined the company in 1936 from Rootes,

was sought. Issigonis was highly regarded by Oak and a measure of this was the fact that the new small-car project was entrusted to him. With two able assistants, Jack Daniels, an expert on chassis and suspension, and Reg Job, a former Pressed Steel employee, who took responsibility for the bodywork, Issigonis had a small but effective team. Wartime projects assumed great importance and the team was forced to di-

The prototype Mosquito, codenamed EX/SX/86, dating from 1943. Note the lack of an opening boot at this stage and the louvred bonnet, an aid to a unique cooling system of the early prototype which adopted a radiator mounted to the rear of the engine block!

vide its efforts between development work on the new car and numerous military machines, including armoured cars, tanks and amphibious motor vehicles.

Spurred on by the enthusiasm of Alec Issigonis and the prospect of a unique opportunity to design a new vehicle from start to finish, they made good progress. From the inspirational sketches provided by Issigonis, Daniels and Job set to work, first producing scale models of the prototype car before progressing to the production of a full-scale prototype vehicle in 1943. Codenamed EX/SX/86, the new model was called the Mosquito. Miles Thomas probably influenced the choice of name, because of his interest in aviation and his experience as a First World War fighter pilot.

Issigonis and Daniels drew on their experience too. They had worked together on the first monocoque design for Morris Motors Limited, the Morris Series M Ten, and their respective wartime projects also involved development work on independent front suspension and torsion bars. They resolved to incorporate these features into the Mosquito, with the addition of rack and pinion steering and smaller 14 inch (36 cm) road wheels to go with the striking styling lines. They were already breaking new ground.

Seeking to have a hand in designing the whole car, Issigonis turned his attention to

EX/SX/86, the Mosquito prototype of 1943, exhibiting what might have been: column gearchange, bench-type front seat and a flat-four engine.

the engine. He favoured the use of an experimental flat-four water-cooled engine, which utilised a three-speed gearbox with column gearchange. 800 cc and 1100 cc versions were later used in the Mosquito and subsequent prototypes. Despite numerous teething problems, both Issigonis and Daniels would have persevered with the flat-four engine and would have preferred to see it used in the production cars. That it did not happen was, as Daniels recalled,

A styling mock-up dating from 1945, showing that the headlamp and grille arrangement had still not been decided upon.

5

Early in the project it was decided that the new small car would be available in saloon and tourer form. This narrow-bodied prototype tourer dates from 1947.

This 1948 pre-production model closely resembles the final styling of the new car. Significantly, it has the wider body with the corresponding 4 inch (10 cm) strip in the bonnet, a split bumper with a concealed fillet and an unusual badge arrangement.

Jack Daniels and Reg Job with the first Morris Minor off the production line and one of the earliest models of the prototype Mosquito.

due to 'inter-factory politics'. The cost of developing a new engine for full-scale production was deemed too great and for practical reasons the engine used in the Series E Morris Eight was slightly modified and used in the first production cars.

Refinements to the prototype cars continued until 1948. In all, eight prototypes were used. Because it was decided to adopt the 918 cc side-valve engine, with the corresponding gearbox, the bench-type front seat and column gearchange were dispensed with and a floor change, with two separate front seats, was incorporated. More significantly, though, there was a momentous eleventh-hour decision by Issigonis to change the dimensions of the car. All the prototypes were 57 inches (145 cm) wide, the same width as the Morris Eight. Issigonis felt that this was too narrow and so he ordered that one of the prototypes be sawn in half lengthways. The two halves were then moved apart and set up at different intervals. At 4 inches (10 cm) apart, Issigonis was satisfied. Reg Job then had to accommodate this additional width:

it required the checking and rechecking of many hundreds of dimensions.

The change had serious implications for the whole design of the car. Apart from the gain in internal dimensions, the main benefit was the increased stability and improved road holding. The body panels had to be modified and the most obvious change was the insertion of an extra 4 inch (10 cm) flat strip in the bonnet — a feature of all subsequent models. There was also the need to add an extra 4 inches to the bumpers. As these had already gone into production on a large scale, they were cut in half and an extra fillet was added to join them together.

With these changes and, at Lord Nuffield's insistence, under the name Morris Minor rather than Mosquito, the first production model, a two-door saloon, was made on 20th September 1948.

The first post-war Motor Show was held in London at Earl's Court in October 1948. Three new Morris models were on display: the Morris Six MS, the Morris Oxford MO and the Morris Minor Series MM. Two-

7

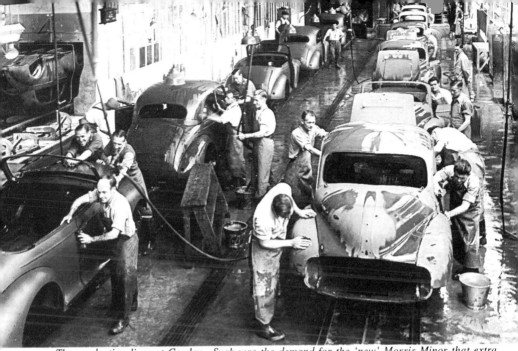

The production lines at Cowley. Such was the demand for the 'new' Morris Minor that extra assembly lines had to be installed.

At the peak of production, 90 per cent of all Morris Minors produced went for export. The top five markets between 1948 and 1960 were Australia, the USA, the Republic of Ireland, South Africa and New Zealand.

The Motor Show car on the Morris Motors stand in October 1948. Although unpretentious, it was the star of the show.

door saloon and tourer versions of the Morris Minor were on show and, much against earlier expectations, it was these models which attracted most attention.

The motoring press was full of praise for the car billed as 'the World's Supreme Small Car'. *Autocar* described it as being 'beyond expectations'. *Motor* claimed that 'it was a car which pleased drivers and passengers alike' and, in a glowing tribute to its designer, went on to say that the car 'approached perfection'.

Road testers also expressed their approval and complimented the road-holding characteristics of the new car, its comfort, tasteful interior design and economical use of fuel. At £358 10s 7d it was competitively priced and, perhaps not surprisingly, demand outstripped supply.

The weak economy of post-war Britain made it essential for exports to take priority over the home market. Over 75 per cent of all Series MM cars produced were exported and there were restrictions in Britain on the purchase of new cars, so acquiring one of these highly rated vehicles was regarded as a major achievement. With the car's popularity undiminished, additional assembly

The striking lines of the Series MM Tourer with side screens detached. This is a much sought-after model, comparatively rare in the United Kingdom.

A left-hand-drive high-headlamp Series MM Tourer, originally exported to Canada but now registered in France. The detachable celluloid side screens which designate this model as a Tourer are in place. This early North American export retains the split bumper.

The later Series MM Convertible dating from 1952, with fixed side windows and a one-piece bumper with overriders and high-headlamp wings.

Right: *The spacious interior of the Series MM four-door saloon, announced in 1950 but initially available only for export.*

Right: *The dependable 918 cc side-valve engine fitted to all Series MM models. Note the roomy engine compartment, a feature which endeared the car to mechanics and do-it-yourself enthusiasts alike.*

Below: *With a top speed of only 62 mph (100 km/h), the desire for increased performance was inevitable. The Alta Car and Engineering Company Limited provided an overhead-valve conversion for the Series MM Minor.*

tracks were laid at Cowley and production was stepped up.

Within months of the start of production, Issigonis and his team had to go back to the drawing board. Impending legislation in the United States laid down new regulations governing the height of headlamps; this meant that the grille-mounted headlamps of the Series MM would have to go. Much to Issigonis's annoyance, the front-end styling had to be modified in order to accommodate the headlamps in the wings. Reg Job, commenting on subsequent attempts to update the shape of the Minor,

11

The earliest venture by a Morris Minor into motor sport was the 1949 Monte Carlo Rally and featured this Series MM. The all-woman crew led by Betty Haig finished second in the Coup des Dames, a creditable performance given the car's lack of basic speed.

claimed that the raising of the headlamps and the resultant change to the front wings 'was all we got away with'!

Although the change was effected as early as December 1948 on a prototype American model, it was not implemented for the whole range until September 1950, when the new four-door Series MM Saloon was introduced. In keeping with the trend, this model was available only for export when it was first launched.

The only other significant changes to the Series MM were the return to a single-piece bumper and valance with the advent of the new-style wings, the additional option of a heater when the engine block was modified to take a water pump, and the change from detachable celluloid side screens on the tourer to fixed glass side windows. With this change, the tourer was redesignated 'convertible'.

The Series MM continued in production until February 1953, by which time a total of 176,002 had been made.

The Morris Minor proved to be a popular choice for club events. This all-Irish team pose with their Series MM Minors before a local event.

12

The distinctive features of the four-door Series II saloon with its honeycomb grille and new-style bonnet motif in period setting.

TO ONE MILLION AND BEYOND

In February 1952 the Nuffield Organisation merged with the Austin Motor Company to form the British Motor Corporation. Given the intense rivalry that existed between Lord Nuffield and Herbert Austin, it seemed an unlikely alliance. However, once established, it made BMC one of the largest motor-manufacturing concerns in Europe.

An immediate consequence for the Morris Minor was the decision to replace the side-valve engine with the more up-to-date 803 cc overhead-valve engine, which had already been fitted to Austin's rival small car, the Austin A30. The change offered improved performance in terms of increased acceleration, with a 0-30 mph (48 km/h) time of 8.4 seconds and a 0-50 mph (80 km/h) time of 25.7 seconds, an improvement on the side-valve of nearly 13 seconds.

While this aspect of the car's performance was to be welcomed, there were doubts about the effectiveness of the gearbox. *Autocar*, in its review of the new

Series II Saloon, lamented the demise of the side-valve close-ratio Morris gearbox, because the new Austin box had less effective synchromesh and gave maximum speeds in second and third gear of only 28 mph (45 km/h) and 42 mph (68 km/h) respectively. In their view, the 'low third gear showed up the modest power output of the engine'.

The only outward sign to denote the advent of the Series II Morris Minor was a change to the badge on the bonnet and the adoption of an 'M' motif.

Two-door and four-door saloons, along with the popular convertibles, remained in production and in October 1953 they were joined by a new model, the Series II Morris Traveller. Unlike the light commercial vehicles, which were introduced in May 1953 and had a separate chassis, the Traveller was made of the same unitary construction as the saloons and convertibles. The wooden ash frame bolted to the steel floorpan and this, in turn, supported an aluminium roof which bolted to the cab.

13

The side panels were also made of aluminium, but the rear wings were steel. In overall length, the Traveller was 1 inch (2.5 cm) longer than the saloon. However, its rear seat folded down to provide a large loading platform, which made it an attractive vehicle for businessmen, commercial travellers and families.

In 1954 the Minor underwent a facelift. The honeycomb grille, so long a feature of the car, was replaced by a slatted grille. This necessitated repositioning the side lights, which now moved to the wing. The rear lamps were redesigned and enlarged to accommodate a bigger reflector. Inside, a new fascia was developed with a centrally placed speedometer and open glove boxes either side.

Further developments followed in 1956. The character of the Minor was changed

The early Series II Traveller was the heaviest Morris Minor even though the side panels, rear door panels and the rear section of the roof were aluminium. Introduced in October 1953, it became one of the most popular variants of the Morris Minor and was one of the last models to be discontinued.

An all-Irish crew led by Bob Noble finished the 1953 Monte Carlo Rally in a factory-supplied Series II Saloon.

when the split windscreen was dispensed with and a single-piece curved screen was fitted. The rear screen was enlarged too and, as a consequence of these changes, the whole of the roof pressing had to be altered. All-round visibility was improved immensely and, with a newly uprated engine and gearbox, the Morris Minor 1000, as it is now known, received a new lease of life.

Engine size was increased to 948 cc. The power output increased by 20 per cent from 30 to 37 brake horsepower and the top speed from 61 to 73 mph (98 to 117 km/h). 0-30 mph (48 km/h) now took only 6.8 seconds and 0-60 mph (97 km/h) was recorded as 30.0 seconds. The gearbox, with a remote-control gearshift, was a great improvement on the previous 803 cc box and

It was customary for all Morris prototype cars to undergo rigorous testing. This included the completion of 10,000 miles (16,000 km) non-stop. This car is the successful Series II model which completed the feat in just over nine days at Goodwood in October 1952.

Above and below: *These striking factory photographs show the clean-cut lines of the front-end revamp of the later Series II models. Note the continued use of trafficators on both models. The convertible pictured is in standard form and would have cost £529 10s 0d in 1956.*

Later Series II Traveller with updated grille arrangement and later owner-added indicators.

The Morris Minor 1000 on the road. Rearward vision is greatly enhanced and there is still a reliance on trafficators. The presence of overriders denotes that this is a de-luxe model.

The millionth Morris Minor to be produced. It was built on 22nd December 1960 and was a landmark in British motoring history. The Morris Minor had become the first British vehicle to reach one million units of production in all its guises.

The 948 cc Traveller variant complete with trafficators but in standard rather than de-luxe specification.

the improved gear ratios allowed for 35 mph (56 km/h) in second and 60.5 mph (95 km/h) in third.

The verdict of contemporary road testers was that the Minor was still 'full of appeal, ahead of its rivals' and that it 'provided for the family man comfort, flexibility and good economy'. Furthermore, 'by using the power and roadholding provided, sports car cornering and acceleration were possible'.

With these improvements, sales continued to increase and the Nuffield export division continued to flourish. The Morris Minor was popular in Britain and elsewhere. The hopes of the original design team and the expectations of the management at Morris Motors that there would be potential for 250,000 units in the short term

had been greatly exceeded and the sales were showing no sign of diminishing.

By December 1960 it was estimated that total sales of all Morris Minor variants were approaching one million. It was decided that in order to mark this significant historical fact a special-edition Morris Minor would be produced. The car, appropriately dubbed the Minor Million, was painted in a delicate shade of lilac and had white gold leather seats, with contrasting black piping. Commemorative Minor Million badges were fitted to the bonnet and boot and special wheel-rim embellishers were added. In all other respects the car was a standard 948 cc Morris Minor.

349 replicas of the 'Million' were produced and, as part of a publicity exercise to mark the fact that the Morris Minor was the

In October 1961 the specifications for the 1962 model year were announced. The semaphore trafficators were replaced by flashing indicators and seat-belt anchorage points were fitted to all models. De-luxe models like the one illustrated had screen washers fitted as standard.

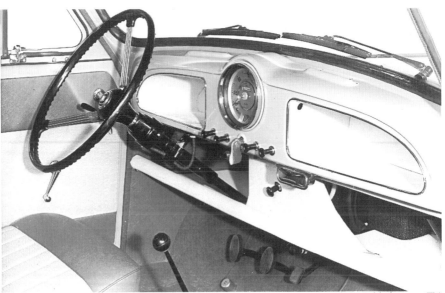

Interior specifications for 1962 changed too. Open glove boxes replaced the lidded ones. This left-hand-drive specification illustrates the simplistic nature of the Morris Minor fascia — an Issigonis trait.

first British vehicle to reach one million units in production, they were sent to distributors in the United Kingdom, Canada, the United States and Europe. Information was embargoed until 4th January 1961 but following this date there was an extensive flurry of publicity.

These cars are the only special-edition Morris Minors and are sought after as collectors' items. Over forty are known to have survived. At the same time BMC attempted to locate the oldest surviving Morris Minor. Provided that it was the oldest surviving model and it had covered at least 100,000 miles (160,000 km), the owner was assured of a new car in exchange for his old one. It was in this way that the first Morris Minor, NWL 576, was discovered and restored to its former glory by BMC apprentices.

Production continued past the one million mark and, in 1962, the Morris Minor received yet another major revamp. This time, the engine size was boosted to 1098 cc. Power output increased to 48 brake horsepower but a change of axle ratio from 4.55 to 4.22 meant that the top speed did not increase beyond the previous 73 mph (117 km/h). Acceleration was further improved, with the 0-60 mph (97 km/h) time bettered by 6 seconds. Other improvements included a larger-diameter clutch, baulk ring synchromesh, larger front brakes and a fresh air heater.

The last batch of improvements came in 1964. Most importantly, the seating was improved, there was a newly designed fascia panel incorporating a lidded glove box on the passenger side, a revised two-spoke safety steering wheel and a combined starter and ignition switch.

By 1966, when sealed beam headlamps were fitted, export sales had begun to dwindle. There was, however, still a thriving market in Britain, not least for the very practical light commercial vehicles.

20

Above and below: *The last of the major updates for the Morris Minor was in October 1962. Performance was transformed by the introduction of the 1098 cc overhead-valve engine. Better brakes and lights were additional features incorporated at this time. The standard saloon (front view) and de-luxe model (rear view) epitomise the final external features of the popular Morris Minor.*

A rare Series II pick-up rescued from a scrapyard and fully restored. This model was introduced in 1953. Passenger seats were an optional extra.

THE LIGHT COMMERCIAL VEHICLES

Light commercial vehicles did not feature in the original line-up of post-war Morris Minor models when they went on public display for the first time at the Earl's Court Motor Show in 1948. It was not until May 1953, under the aegis of the newly formed British Motor Corporation (BMC), that the Morris Minor Quarter Ton Van and Pick-up models were announced and the process of phasing out their predecessors, the Morris Eight-based 5 cwt (254 kg) vans (Z Series), began. Though termed the O-type Quarter Ton Van and Pick-up, the new models shared much of the styling and almost all of the mechanical specifications of the already established Series II saloons. For this reason, these early models are more commonly referred to as Series II vans and pick-ups.

Much was made of the compactness, versatility and economy of the new models, which were available in three options: complete van, complete pick-up with or without canvas tilt, and a cab/chassis with the

facility for coachbuilders to add custom-made bodies. Powered by the 803 cc overhead-valve engine and designed with an all-steel box-sectioned full-length chassis, the commercials sold well.

Boosted by pre-production orders from the General Post Office for specially designed Post Office vans and telephone engineers' vans, Series II light commercial vehicle (LCV) sales exceeded 48,000 in just over three years. During this time, the LCVs had, like the rest of the Morris Minor range, undergone some restyling. In October 1954 a new-style fascia with a centrally mounted speedometer and a redesigned front grille panel with repositioned side lights were introduced. Two years later the Morris Minor 1000 range was announced. These new models had even more new styling features, including the end of the split windscreen. Most important, however, was the introduction of a much needed uprated power unit. In terms of power and acceleration, the 803 cc engine and corresponding

22

Series II Post Office vans were fitted with rubber wings and had an opening windscreen.

transmission could not have been said to have been a resounding success and so the introduction of the much livelier and smoother 948 cc engine and gearbox was a welcome, if somewhat overdue, innovation. Morris Minor 1000 sales boomed. By 1962 a hundred thousand 948 cc LCVs had rolled off the production lines and total Morris Minor sales had surpassed one million.

In late 1962 the engine size of the Morris Minor was increased still further. It was now powered by the 1098 cc unit and further styling refinements were introduced, enhancing the appeal of all the vehicles. For the LCVs the additional power provided the scope for increasing the payload from 5 to 6 cwt (254 to 305 kg) — so making them more attractive to potential

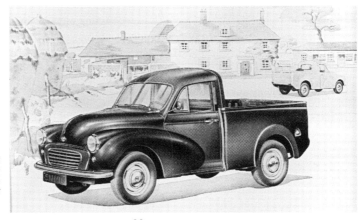

Artwork from the 1955 advertising brochure for the later Series II pick-up.

23

customers. It signalled the end of the Quarter Ton series commercials and prompted the advertising personnel to promote the new Morris 6 cwt Series III van as 'the world's biggest small van buy'.

In 1968 the payload was increased to 8 cwt (406 kg) and rear springs were modified to take an extra leaf. The suspension was uprated to cope with the anticipated extra loading. 6 cwt (305 kg) versions remained in production alongside these new models. By this time BMC had been superseded by British Leyland and, under the control of Lord Stokes, Morris Minor vans and pick-ups were produced and marketed with Austin badging. Distinguishing features of these products of badge engineering were a crinkle-type slatted grille, Austin badges in the centre of the steering wheel and on the bonnet and Austin hubcaps.

The last of the LCVs was produced in 1971 at Adderley Park, Birmingham, and, although production records were destroyed, it is estimated that in all 326,626 Morris Minor light commercial vehicles were made.

Of this total, some 50,000 were specially ordered by the GPO to be used as mail vans and as telephone engineers' vans. With so many in service over the years, Morris Minor Post Office vans became a familiar sight throughout the British Isles and the Channel Islands. Many remained in service long after production ceased and at least one van was still in use in 1982 in the livery of British Telecom.

The special features of the GPO vehicles, which distinguish them from the rest of the LCVs made during a production run which

spanned nineteen years, are less familiar. The very early Post Office vehicles are scarce today. They had the distinction of being fitted with rubber wings which had headlamps mounted on top. There were few comforts for the average postman in those days: there was one seat and no heater — though there was the option of additional ventilation by means of the opening windscreen! Series III Post Office vehicles followed more conventional styling but are still easily identifiable with, among other things, the rather unusual security arrangements on the driver's door, which used a Yale lock.

Apart from the GPO, many metropolitan and municipal authorities were fleet users of Morris Minor commercial vehicles. Service industries, wholesalers, retailers, farmers, builders and countless other tradesmen found the claims of the sales literature to be true:

'There was a need for a Morris Quarter Ton or pick-up in any type of business. Grocers, newsagents, radio and television engineers, florists, seedsmen, wine and spirit merchants, dry cleaners, ironmongers, milliners and bakers were indeed just a few of the widely differing trades that found that the Morris Quarter Ton vehicles would provide a light, rapid delivery service at low cost!'

During the years of production, there was little else seriously to rival the versatility and economy of these popular workhorses, a fact borne out by the GPO's long-standing contract. For the operator who preferred to have his own particular coachbuilt body fitted to his vehicles, the option of a cab/chassis was available. Gown vans, garage

The Post Office was one of the main customers for the Morris Minor light commercials. This Royal Mail van is one of the last produced.

breakdown and recovery pick-ups, ice-cream vans and even specially adapted delivery vans for Esso Blue and Aladdin pink paraffin all used the Morris Minor chassis to good effect.

Not all the non-standard commercials were commissioned at the whim of individual owners. An extra-large van was manufactured in Denmark by the importing company, DOMI. With a single rear door and extra length and height, its overall capacity was considerably increased. In spite of this and the innovative features, these models, which were produced to Series II and Series III specification, remained a Danish option only.

These popular classic light commercial vehicles are still in use by some commercial enterprises today — a testimony to the enduring qualities of Sir Alec Issigonis's design and the durability and popularity of the Morris Minor.

Austin variants of the Morris Minor van were produced. They were distinguishable by their crinkle-type grille and Austin badging on the bonnet.

This page: *Morris Minors being assembled at the Molenaar factory in Holland, where, in keeping with company policy, locally produced components were used. These included glass, tyres, paint and electrical items.*

26

Crates of CKD Minors at the Molenaar Company in Holland awaiting assembly.

PRODUCTION OVERSEAS

In the motor-manufacturing industry CKD, which stands for completely knocked down, is the system where vehicles are shipped abroad in component form, in easily transportable packing cases ready for assembly in the market for which they are destined. This method of car assembly represented a major segment of Morris Minor production during, and indeed beyond, the period of 22 years when Morris Minors were in production in Britain.

The boom years were in the early 1950s, when it was imperative for both economic and social reasons to rebuild and expand the British economy following the disruption of the war years. For many it was an austere time, with rationing still part of everyday life, but it was also a time of optimism, and especially so in the motor industry, where every company was seeking to expand its business. At Cowley in Oxford a new factory was built to accommodate the increasing demands of the export market for the CKD models. Personnel were specially trained to assist with the establishment of overseas assembly plants and in the Cowley works itself there was even a demonstration bay where overseas personnel could study every aspect of assembly with standard Nuffield jigs and equipment with the assistance of experienced assembly foremen and technologists.

In countries such as Australia, New Zealand, South Africa, India, Holland, Denmark and the Republic of Ireland special plants were opened and fully equipped to do the assembly work. Standard jigs, tools and fixtures were supplied and special arrangements entered into for the supply of local materials for some components such as glass, batteries, tyres, upholstery and interior fittings. While the objective was to produce a vehicle to the same specification as the British-assembled product, the priority was to reduce costs and make use of local materials where possible. This obviously extended to the use of local labour.

The attractions of this method of production are substantial, but the logistics of supplying all the necessary components were considerable, especially as there were 19,587 separate parts for one Morris Minor.

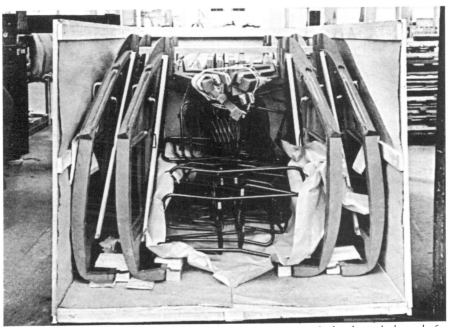

There is not a millimetre of wasted space as components are meticulously packed, ready for dispatch.

So the Nuffield operation had to be well organised. Packaging had to be as compact as possible to save on shipping costs and delivery schedules had to be tightly observed to avoid contravening local tariff deadlines in the various ports of entry.

Success helped guarantee the advertising department's claim that the Morris Minor was indeed 'the World's Supreme Small Car'.

In Ireland the cars were assembled by G. A. Brittain in Dublin. Records show that the first CKD Morris Minors dispatched for export all went to Ireland. Eighteen Series MM saloons were sent in 1948, making Ireland the first overseas country to have Morris Minor production. In succeeding years, G. A. Brittain assembled all versions of the Series MM but, after the Series II models were introduced, they restricted their production mainly to two-door and four-door saloons with a small number of convertible models.

Brittain continued with production until 1971 and, like the Cowley factory, finished production by assembling a two-door saloon. However, some time after this car was sold, the company decided to use all the parts that remained to build another car to display in their showroom. The result was a four-door saloon finished in 'teal' blue with a matching light blue interior. This car is now unique, because it has never been registered for use on the road and has always been carefully looked after. G. A. Brittain went into liquidation in 1975 and the car was sold to Ken Smith, who kept it until 1985, when the current owner, Paul Hanley, acquired it. The car is still unlicensed and is used only occasionally.

The car exhibits the features that were unique to Morris Minors assembled in Ireland. Unlike the British cars, the grille and the road wheels are painted in the body colour and the wing piping, which is normally matched to body colour, is black on

28

all Irish models. The interior fitting differs slightly with the most noticeable difference being the plain door trims as opposed to the heat-formed trim associated with late models. The most striking feature, which led some British owners to doubt the car's authenticity, is the evidence of major welding across the bulkhead, clear evidence of its CKD origin.

Another country that was a major producer of Morris Minors was Holland. One saloon was assembled in 1949 in a factory owned by the Molenaar Company at Jutphaas but, after this, production was stepped up and in 1953 a much bigger factory was built at Amersfoort. However, only two-door and four-door saloon versions of the Series MM were produced in Holland.

The Dutch company, Molenaar, was ideally suited to take on Morris Minor production. They had previously been producing MGs since 1932 and had added Morris models to their output in 1936. In addition they already had their own established suppliers of components, such as windows from Staalglas, tyres from Vredestein, lighting equipment from Philips and paint from Valspar. The provision of such parts helped keep costs down at the point of entry into Holland. This was vital because in 1951 no car could be imported into Holland if it cost more than the Dutch equivalent of £420. The Dutch vehicles had left-hand drive and so there were some major differences from the British-made cars but, like the complete left-hand-drive cars exported to the United States, Dutch CKD models had the annoying feature of only one door lock (for all but the latest models). This was supplied as for right-hand-drive vehicles, so, to get into the car, the driver had first to open the passenger door, unlock the driver's door

from the inside and then walk around the car to get in!

Production at the Amersfoort plant continued until 1966, at which time Morris Minors were no longer imported.

It was at about this time, too, that production ceased at the DOMI (Dansk Oversoisk Motor Industri) factory in Denmark. DOMI was a well established company when Morris Minor production began and was an obvious potential choice for CKD. The vehicles produced have some interesting features, including modifications to the engine ancillaries to make starting easier in the winter months. Like the later Irish cars, Danish Morris 1000 models have plain door trims. However, the most interesting omission from all Danish Morris Minors is the famous bonnet motif, which was banned on the grounds of safety. However, the early-type bonnet flash used on Series MM models and on some commercial vehicles was acceptable.

Another important market for CKD models was Australia. Here, too, local preferences in bodywork were approved, as were a number of other features, including paint colours and types, perhaps partly because of the climate and partly because Australia was the largest export market. However, not all the Morris Minor vehicles were assembled at the New South Wales plant, as many of the early models were imported as complete cars.

New Zealand had a thriving assembly factory at the Dominions Motor Plant in Auckland. Production continued there until 1974, after Morris Minors had ceased to be made in Britain.

Many plants in other countries received and assembled CKD Morris Minors. Their employees, like the workers on the production lines in Britain, played their part in the success of the Morris Minor.

Left: *The Morris Minor was used by a number of police forces, including the Metropolitan Police. Resplendent in Bermuda blue and white, police Minors sported an unusual feature, a zipped headlining. This was to allow access to the roof-mounted 'Police' sign.*

Right: *This is the final format of the Morris Minor interior. With heat-formed trim panels, much more comfortable seats and steering-column locks on the last of the commercials and Travellers, attempts were being made to keep up with the times.*

THE FINAL YEARS

During the late 1960s Morris Minor sales declined steadily. In 1968, when Leyland and BMC merged to form British Leyland, annual production dropped to 31,640. Although many people expected that as a result of the merger Lord Stokes would discontinue production of the Morris Minor immediately, it was not until June 1969 that the first step towards phasing out the Morris Minor was taken when the last convertible was produced.

Competition was fierce in the late 1960s. Even within the newly formed British Leyland group the Minor faced a stiff challenge from the new Austin Maxi and, more importantly, from the popular Austin/Morris 1100/1300 range. With plans advanced for a new Morris model — the Marina — it seemed only a matter of time before production would finally cease at Cowley. The grim realisation that the profit margin on each Morris Minor produced in 1968 was

in single figures, together with the diminishing sales market, resulted in the production of saloons being discontinued at Cowley on 12th November 1970 in order to make way for the new Marina production lines. In April of the following year the last Traveller was assembled at the Morris Commercial Cars Plant at Adderley Park, Birmingham, thus bringing to an end a production run for the Morris Minor which spanned 22 years.

In all, 1.6 million Morris Minors had been produced. As the first British car whose production had exceeded one million, it had secured a place in motoring history. More importantly, Alec Issigonis, knighted in 1969, had designed a vehicle capable of being updated while still retaining its essential character. He also designed a car which outlasted many of its contemporaries and which is held in high regard by discerning motorists all over the world.

The convertible model was the first to be discontinued. The last convertible is seen here at Stewart and Ardern of Staines, Surrey, where Walter Lorch, chairman of the Elga Group of Companies, took delivery of it. He is seen here behind the wheel of his Austin Ten Tourer (1935), one of several vintage cars in his collection.

The end of the line. Here, the last two-door saloon is seen on 12th November 1970, the day when production of the Minor ceased at Cowley after 22 years.

FURTHER READING

Allen, Michael. *British Family Cars of the Fifties*. Haynes, 1985.
Allen, Michael. *British Family Cars of the Early Sixties*. Haynes, 1989.
Horvat, Max. *Magnificent Morris Minor*. Bookmarque, 1990.
Newell, Ray. *Morris Minor and 1000* (Super Profile series). Haynes/Foulis, 1982.
Newell, Ray. *Series MM Morris Minor* (Super Profile series). Haynes/Foulis, 1984.
Newell, Ray. *Morris Minor – The First Fifty Years*. Bay View, 1997.
Pender, Karen. *Secret Life of the Morris Minor*. Veloce, 1996.
Practical Classics Traveller Restoration. Kelsey Publishing, 1992.
Robson, Graham. *The Cars of BMC*. Motor Racing Publications, 1987.
Skilleter, Paul. *The World's Supreme Small Car*. Osprey, third edition 1989.
Tyler, Jim. *Morris Minor Restoration, Preparation, Maintenance*. Osprey, 1995.
Young, Philip. *The Himalayan Minor*. Speedwell Books, 1987.

PLACES TO VISIT

Heritage Motor Centre, Banbury Road, Gaydon, Warwickshire CV35 0BJ. Telephone: 01926 641188.
Museum of British Road Transport, St Agnes Lane, Hales Street, Coventry CV1 1PN. Telephone: 01203 832425.
National Motor Museum, John Montagu Building, Beaulieu, Brockenhurst, Hampshire SO42 7ZN. Telephone: 01590 612345.

CLUB
The Morris Minor Owners Club, 127-9 Green Lane, Derby DE1 1RZ.

The revival of interest in classic saloon-car racing has generated renewed enthusiasm for the Morris Minor in the 1990s. Robin Moore has been one of the more successful drivers in the championship for pre-1957 cars.